Kings and Queens for God

CAROL GREENE

ILLUSTRATED BY
LYDIA HALVERSON

Augsburg
MINNEAPOLIS

Family Read-Aloud Collection
Foreword by Walter Wangerin, Jr.
VOL. II

KINGS AND QUEENS FOR GOD

Cover design by Craig P. Claeys
Text design by Lois Stanfield, LightSource Images

_____

Library of Congress Cataloging-in-Publication Data

ISBN 0-8066-3612-2

_____

The paper used in this publication meets the minimum requirements of American National Standard for Information Sciences—Permanence of Paper for Printed Library Materials, ANSI Z329.48-1984.

_____

Manufactured in Singapore   AF 9-3612

02   01   00   99   98   1   2   3   4   5   6   7   8   9   10

Contents

Worlds to Share: Foreword by Walter Wangerin, Jr.   iv

The King with the Blazing Faith—*Oswald of Northumbria*   1

A Plague of Poets—*Guaire Aidni of Ireland*   9

The Emperor and a Grubby
    Little Churchman—*Charlemagne of the Franks*   17

The King Who Was Beaten
    with a Broom—*Alfred the Great of Wessex*   25

A Prince's Choice—*Vladimir of Russia*   33

Too Good to Be King—*Edward the Confessor of England*   41

The Princess Who Wanted the World—*Matilda of Scotland*   49

Flowers in the Snow—*Elizabeth of Hungary*   57

The Princess and the Dragon—*Jadwiga of Poland*   65

"Till Death Us Do Part"—*Katarina of Sweden*   73

The Girl Who Married the
    Terrible Tsar—*Anastasia Romanov of Russia*   81

An Old-Fashioned Queen—*Maria Theresa of Austria*   89

The Plain Princess—*Leopoldina of Brazil*   97

When a Princess Said, "No"—*Victoria of England*   105

The Disobedient Chief—*Khama of Bechuanaland*   113

FOREWORD

Worlds to Share

WALTER WANGERIN, JR.

ow often I wished I could companion my children through their most difficult experiences—or through their every joy. Too often I learned of the twists of their personal journeys after the fact. I hadn't been there. Moreover, if I had been, I may have been denied full access to—a full understanding of—their hearts and minds in the event.

But there is a way, a blessed way, into the hearts and minds of our children as they journey through life. When the parent reads out loud to the child, the older one becomes the younger one's most intimate companion. They travel together through dangers and delights, through adventures and mysteries, through stories, through genuine experiences—through life itself.

The power of a story well told is to create whole experiences for the child, but controlled experiences with beginnings and middles, and with good endings.

The reward for parents who read such stories to their children is an intimacy that is emotional, spiritual, and real. The walls come down; nothing is hidden between them.

And the benefits to children are legion:

- They are assured that, whatever the experience, they are not alone.

- They are fearless before the circumstances of the story, however frightening or thrilling. And, in consequence, they are prepared to meet similar circumstances in their real life with the boldness and trust that come of experience.

- They, when they laugh heartily, are empowered! For the laughter of children in the face of giants or troubles or evils is their sense of superiority. Their ability to see silliness in danger is their freedom to take spiritual steps above the danger.

- And they are granted a genuine independence, a freedom of choice. For children can choose to hear a fantasy tale as fantasy only, something fun and funny, but not anything you would meet in the real world. And they can listen to stories of distant heroes and heroic deeds as ancient history and nothing to do with their life. Or else they can choose to identify completely with the main character—in which case this fantasy or this ancient story stands for things absolutely real in their own world. Children don't make such choices consciously; they make them in the deep parts of their souls, when they are ready to take the real ride of the story. And the fact that they can and do choose grants them true personhood.

And you, their parent, are there, companioning your child through wonders and terrors, through friendships and wisdom, through experience into experience.

When my father bought a thick book containing all the tales of Hans Christian Andersen and read them to us, he did me a kindness more profound than mere entertainment. He began to weave a world that genuinely acknowledged all the monsters in mine, as well as all the ridiculous situations and silly asides that I as a child found significant. Dad/Andersen was my whispering, laughing, wise companion when I most needed companionship.

Night after night my dad would read a story in his articulate, baritone voice. Gently the voice invited me. Slowly I accepted the invitation and delivered myself to a wonderful world. And as I looked around, I discovered that this world was confident with solutions, and I was a citizen of some authority and reputation. I was no longer alone, no longer helpless.

Dad would sit in a chair beside my bed, one lamp low at his shoulder, his pipe clamped between his teeth and sending the smell of his presence and his affections to me where I lay. Mostly the room, an attic with slanted ceilings, was in darkness. The wind whistled in the eaves.

"Ready?" Dad would say.

We would nod. We would curl tight beneath the covers.

"Once upon a time," Dad would read, sending me straight through the attic walls into the night, onto the wind, for gorgeous, breathtaking flights.

What part of my being could not find affirmation in such an event? My body was present, delighting in its vicarious adventures. All my senses were alert and active, sight and sound and smell and touch. My emotions were given every opportunity—highs so tremendously high, and lows acceptable because Dad was the leader. My mind, my intellect, labored at solutions before the story itself declared them.

And all my affections were granted lovely objects. I could love in that event when my father read to us: I could love characters in the tale; I could love their qualities, their deeds, their struggles; I could love the tale itself—but mostly, I could love my father, whose very voice was his offering of love to me. We were one in this event, one in the reading and in the listening and in the experiencing.

Night after night my father read to us from that thick book. Night after night I lived the adventures that gave order to my turbulent child's experience. The tales gave shape to my waking self, to my instincts, to my faith in God, and to my adulthood yet to come. For I am what I am now, in part, because once I experienced important events within the protected sphere of my father's dear influence.

These events were deep and primal.

But on the page they were merely stories—until my father opened his mouth and read them to me.

The King with the Blazing Faith

OSWALD OF NORTHUMBRIA
A.D. 604–642

 ow can the spark of faith spring up in a land, a family, a person continually surrounded by betrayal, bloodshed and hate? Eleven-year-old Oswald didn't seem to stand a chance.

Oswald's father was Ethelfrid (EHTH-ehl-frihd) the Ravager, who took the throne of the British kingdom of Northumbria from his brother-in-law, Edwin. But Edwin returned, killed Ethelfrid, and exiled Oswald and his brothers to Scotland. That's where they met the monks of Iona (eye-OH-nah) and learned from them about Jesus. Soon they were all baptized.

Years passed and the spark of faith burned steadily stronger in Oswald. Then the fierce Welsh king, Cadwallon (kad-WAHL-lunn), killed Edwin and called Oswald's two older brothers to govern Northumbria under him. They thought Cadwallon would like them better if they weren't Christians, so they denied their faith. Cadwallon was not impressed; within a year he killed them both.

Back in Scotland, Oswald's heart yearned for the people of Northumbria, his people. They deserved better than to be ruled by the cruel Cadwallon. Oswald couldn't put together much of an army, but he did his best and felt sure he was doing God's will. Then, armed with faith, he made his move.

Oswald and his little army crossed the Scottish border one day in 634 and marched to a place near Hexham and Rowley Burn. Although he knew that Cadwallon's soldiers were near and greatly outnumbered his own forces, Oswald showed no sign of fear.

"Tomorrow we will engage in battle," he told his men. "But this evening I want you to build a cross, a huge wooden cross like that on which our Savior died."

When the cross was finished, he had the men dig a hole and place the base of the cross in it. Then, with his own hands, Oswald held the cross steady while the hole was refilled.

"Now," he cried to his army, "let us kneel down together and pray to the only true and all-powerful God to defend us from our fierce enemy. For God knows that we fight a just war, a war to save our country."

Only a few of Oswald's soldiers were Christians, but none of them could resist the faith that burned in his eyes and rang in his voice. So they all knelt down and prayed.

That night Oswald had a dream in which he saw Columba, the great saint who had converted so many in Scotland. In the dream, Columba stretched out his cloak until it sheltered all of Oswald's sleeping soldiers and promised that they would be victorious the next day.

At dawn Oswald led his men into battle and saw his dream come true. Cadwallon was killed, and his army fell apart, each soldier running for his life. From then on, the place of battle was known as "The Heavenly Field" (later "Heavenfield").

Oswald had no trouble taking the throne of Northumbria after that. In fact, the people welcomed him with open arms. But as far as Oswald was concerned, his battle had only begun. He had not intended merely to free his people from Cadwallon's yoke. He wanted to give them the gift of faith in Jesus that had so illuminated his own life.

Oswald knew, though, that he couldn't accomplish such a task by himself. So he sent word to the monks of Iona to ask them for help. The monks promptly sent one of their number to serve as a missionary. He didn't stay long.

"Those English have no manners!" he stormed when he returned to Iona. "They behave like *savages*."

"They did not respond gladly to your message of the gospel?" asked one of the other monks as they sat in council.

"Respond gladly? They are the most stubborn, barbarous, and uncivilized people I have ever seen!"

"Oh dear," said the other monks.

"What can we do about them?" asked one.

"Savagery and stubbornness are not easy barriers to overcome," said another.

"And yet we must bring them the good news of Christ," added a third. "Surely they need it as much as anyone."

Then a priest, known for his wisdom and gentleness, spoke up. "Perhaps, my brother," he said to the missionary, "you were a little too harsh for such primitive people. Perhaps they require softer handling. Let them taste the milk of the faith before giving them its meat. Show them the gentle, accepting Christ before you become strict."

"Indeed, Father Aidan (AY-duhn)!" cried the other monks. "You are right! And who better than you, the mildest of us all, to be their missionary?"

So they consecrated Aidan a bishop and sent him off with some helpers to convert the crude folk of Northumbria. Oswald was delighted to see him.

Now Aidan, originally a native of Ireland, spoke only Gaelic (GAY-lihk), while the Northumbrian people spoke only English.

But Oswald did not see why that should be a problem. Aidan would eventually learn English, and meanwhile, Oswald spoke both languages and could serve as the bishop's interpreter. So what if he had to put aside some other kingly duties to follow Aidan around? Surely the work they did together was the most important of all.

It did not take long for that work to bear fruit. People could not help but pay attention to Aidan. Not only was he a gentleman, but he seemed to understand them—rich and poor alike—down to the bottom of their souls. And if their manners were not always as smooth and polished as they should be—well, Aidan didn't seem to think any the less of them for it. Combine the presence of such a great man with that of their own king, whose faith in Christ no one could doubt, and it was no wonder more and more Northumbrians turned to Jesus.

Oswald soon realized that Aidan would need a home base in Northumbria where he and his helpers could continue to follow their monastic rituals. So he gave the bishop the island of Lindisfarne, which was so close to the Northumbrian coast that at low tide the monks could walk back and forth. But Aidan did more than live and worship on Lindisfarne. He established a school for Northumbrian boys there, some of whom grew up to be leaders in the church.

Meanwhile, Oswald's influence was also spreading. Instead of just king of Northumbria, he became known as a "bretwalda" (BREHT-wall-duh), a ruler of Britain. This was not really a political title, since the English provinces would not be united for hundreds of years. Rather "bretwalda" was an ancient, honorary title awarded to a king whose influence and prestige spread beyond his own realm and overshadowed that of his fellow kings.

Such prestige, though, did not go to Oswald's head. By this time he was so filled with the love of Christ that he hardly even thought of himself. All his concern was for his people. Did the monks have enough money to build more churches? Were sick people getting the care they needed? Were poor people getting enough to eat?

One Easter Day, Oswald and Aidan sat down together to enjoy a feast. A huge silver dish of fine food was set before the king, and the bishop was about to say grace when a servant rushed into the hall.

"Sire," he said to Oswald, "I am sorry to interrupt, but a large crowd of poor people has gathered in the street. They have come from all over, certain that you will not refuse them aid on this holy day."

"Of course I will not refuse them!" declared Oswald. "Take this food from the table and divide it among them. Take the silver dish, too. Break it into pieces and give it to them as well."

Aidan was most impressed. He took the king's right hand and raised it. "May this hand never perish," he said.

Oswald also saw prayer as one of his kingly duties, one that he performed each night from midnight till dawn. In fact, he spent so much time praying for his people that even when he was doing other things, it looked as if he were praying.

During one period, a terrible plague broke out among the people. Scores died, and those who didn't trembled with fear that they or someone they loved would be next. Oswald's heart ached for them, and he fell down on his knees.

"Merciful God," he prayed, "take pity on these poor people. Let me and my family be taken in their place if that might stop this dreadful pestilence."

Oswald did fall ill, and for a time it looked as if his prayer would be answered. A deep peace settled over him as he thought that God was willing to accept his life for the lives of his beloved subjects.

But then three angels appeared beside his bed.

"God heard your prayer, Oswald," they said. "The plague will end. But it is not time for you to die, and you shall recover."

And that is exactly what happened. The plague ended and Oswald recovered.

It was not long, though, before Oswald faced another enemy. In spite of his hard work—and that of Aidan and the monks—at spreading the gospel, many people in England still clung to their heathen beliefs. Among them was Penda, king of Mercia. Penda despised the work Oswald was doing and hungered for the territory Oswald ruled. So he joined forces with Welsh soldiers and began his attacks.

Penda met Oswald at a place called Maserfield. Once again, Oswald had a much smaller army, and this time they were not able to prevail. Oswald fought with them, and as he saw his men dying around him and felt himself falling, his heart was wrenched with pity, and he called out a prayer for his soldiers: "Lord, have mercy on their souls!"

Soon everyone in Northumbria knew that Oswald's last breath had been a prayer for his people. They were so moved by this that, for years to come, if someone saw people in distress, he would say, "Lord have mercy on their souls!" as Oswald said when he fell.

*O*swald *was thirty-eight years old when he died in 642. He had ruled Northumbria for just nine years. But during those years and the years that followed, his blazing faith lit other sparks of faith, not only in his beloved Northumbria, but in lands as far away as Germany and Italy.*

Penda continued to attack Northumbria during the reign of Oswald's cousin, Oswin. But in 655, another cousin, Oswy, defeated Penda's army and killed the pagan ruler. And Mercia, Penda's kingdom, at once accepted the Christian faith.

Talk about It

- Talk about some people who have inspired you with their faith. They might be people whom you know today—even family members—or people who helped you realize that you wanted to be a Christian.

- Who are the "savage and stubborn" people today who need to hear the good news about Jesus? Talk about ways your family could help them hear it.

Prayer

Make a list of people you know (or know about) who especially need God's help right now. Spend a few moments silently thinking about and praying for each of them. Then conclude together with Oswald's words: "Lord, have mercy on their souls."

A Plague of Poets

GUAIRE AIDNI OF IRELAND
SEVENTH CENTURY

*S*eventh-century Ireland stretched green and unbroken from the rocky coast of the Atlantic to the Irish Sea. Roads led to no bustling towns, but to hill-forts, monasteries, or lonely homesteads where people grew crops and grazed animals.

The country was divided roughly into five provinces, each with its own king and often several lesser kings or tribal chieftains under him.

But separated as the Irish people were geographically and politically, a number of things bound them together. Their ancient Celtic (KEL-tik) heritage had instilled in them a deep love of nature and of learning. When Saint Patrick came to teach Christianity in 432, he built on these loves.

The Irish people also shared a strong oral tradition. Rules told by one generation to the next were sometimes known as the Brehon (BREE-hon) Law. These rules covered family and tribal loyalty, ownership of property, election of kings, and many other aspects of daily life. The Brehon Law also covered hospitality.

Perhaps because of their isolation, the Irish people realized how important it was to welcome strangers. As Christianity spread, they saw more reasons to be hospitable. "Christ is in the person of every guest," they said.

Ireland's greatest model of hospitality came in a seventh-century king, Guaire (GWAYR) Aidni (AYD-nee) of Connaught (cuh-NAWT).

THE WHOLE COURT OF KING GUAIRE hustled and bustled like a colony of ants. So much to do! So many preparations to make! Would they ever be finished in time?

The poet Senchan (SEHN-kuhn) Torpeist (TOHR-pay-ihst) was coming to visit. Now, a visit from any poet was cause for extensive preparations and great joy. But Senchan! Why, he was known and admired the length and breadth of Ireland—the greatest poet of the times.

There was just one little problem, mused King Guaire as he tried to keep out of everyone's way. With most poets you knew where you stood. The laws were clear. If the poet intended to stay only one night, he was allowed to bring twenty-four attendants with him. If he planned to stay longer or if additional company was expected for a feast, the number of attendants allowed was reduced to ten.

Word had it, though, that Senchan, along with some other important poets, considered himself above these laws. He traveled with as many attendants as he liked, fully expecting them all to be welcomed and looked after.

"And I *want* to welcome and look after them," Guaire said to himself. "But, dear God, how many will there be?"

He soon had his answer as, with much noise and fanfare, Senchan Torpeist and his party arrived. There was Senchan himself and 150 lesser poets who basked in their master's glow. Then there were 150 students who were learning to become poets. And each of the lesser poets and each of the students had a servant and a dog. There were also, of course, a great many wives, not to mention horses.

Guaire must have taken a very deep breath and then another before he said to himself, "I can do it. I can welcome and look after them all. Christ is in the person of every guest. Every stranger is Christ. Dear God, help me!"

At last evening came, and all the guests were somehow settled in. Senchan sat beside Guaire at dinner and shared with him the special haunch of meat reserved for the king. Firelight flickered on the walls, and it was time for the poet to perform. Guaire leaned back, his hands on his stomach, and prepared to enjoy himself.

Of what would Senchan tell? Would it be one of the great epics that recounted Ireland's history? Every good poet had memorized at least 350 of these and could perform them brilliantly. Or would it be a new poem, composed by Senchan himself, recounting the events of a recent battle in some other province?

"It is a huge job these poets have," thought Guaire. Crammed into their heads was all the history of the past as well as the news of the present. They could tell the genealogy of every important family in Ireland and recite all the Irish laws, too. Champions and kings, beautiful women, and nature—all were the stuff of which they fashioned their poems—and in rhyme, too, glorious rhyme that teased the ear as it satisfied the heart.

No wonder poets had to study so long, a minimum of twelve years, and sometimes much longer. No wonder some of them were as rich as kings—or even richer. They deserved their rewards. And Senchan, too, would be rewarded richly.

Ah! Now Senchan picked up his harp and began to strum the slow, steady notes that would sound under the words of his poems. But what was this? He wasn't recounting a historical event or to-day's news. Instead, Senchan, wise poet that he was, was making up a poem right here on the spot—a poem in praise of Guaire himself.

Guaire couldn't help smiling, although he tried to look grave and dignified. Senchan's poem said many fine things about him. It made him out to be a much better fellow than he knew he was.

But sometimes a person needed that sort of praise, especially a king.

The price for such a poem, Guaire remembered, was three milk-cows. But no. That was for a lower grade of poet. For Senchan the price would be more. Well, never mind. Guaire would see that he got his fair price and then double it. What a truly excellent poet he was! And, with luck, Guaire and his court could look forward to at least a week of evenings of poetry. A poet of Senchan's stature would never come for just one day.

A month passed and Guaire reveled in all the marvelous poetry he and his court were hearing. Then a second month went by, and a third, and three more. Guaire began to count his cattle. How dreadful he would feel if he ran out of food! After nine months, most of Ireland had heard about what was happening to poor Guaire.

"Over six hundred people he has been feeding and housing all this while," folks marveled. "How long will it be before he runs out of food?"

"He'll have to send them away soon," said some.

"Not Guaire the Hospitable," said others. "He'd give them his last crust before he'd send them away."

"He must know what can happen to a king who gets on the wrong side of a poet," said the first group. "Some very nasty poems have been composed about kings like that. Those poems shame not only the king, but his children and their children, too."

"That's not why Guaire continues his kindness to Senchan and his troupe," said the king's supporters. "The man has the heart of a saint. He truly believes he is entertaining Christ in each person of that horde."

"Well, Christ had better send him help pretty soon. Guaire is only a mortal man, and mortal men can do only so much."

By the time a year had passed, Guaire felt the cold hand of fear close around his heart. "Dear Father in heaven," he prayed, "dear Lord Christ, and dear Holy Ghost our Comforter, I do need help. It's not for myself that I mind running out of cattle. Gladly will I sell everything I own to buy more food. Gladly will I starve myself. But what of them, your dear poets, Lord? What of the servants who tend them so they may practice their art? What of the wives, the horses, and the dogs? Oh, Lord, it will break my heart if I have nothing more to offer them!"

At last, words of Guaire's predicament reached even his brother, Marban, who was a holy man and a hermit. Marban was horrified.

"God sent plagues of locusts and frogs on Egypt to break Pharaoh's pride," he thought. "But my poor brother, as generous a man as ever lived, has done nothing to deserve this plague of poets."

It did not take Marban long to come up with a plan to rescue Guaire. He set out immediately for his brother's home and stood before the poet.

"Senchan Torpeist!" he declared. "Most noble of Ireland's poets, most gifted and wise! For you and for those whose lights are but reflections of your greater light, I have a commission—nay, a quest for which only one such as yourself is qualified."

Senchan looked interested.

"For countless years," continued Marban, "the ancient tale 'The Cattle-raid of Cooley' has been lost to us. For countless years no Irish poet has sung it and no Irish ears have heard it. What a pity, what a tragedy to lose such an important part of our history. Tradition says, as you no doubt know, Senchan, that 'The Cattle-raid of Cooley' was carried east over the sea. I have reason to believe that tradition speaks truly. And I also believe that if any man can find the epic and bring it back to us, that man, Senchan, is you."

Senchan looked more than interested. He looked eager.

"And so," continued Marban, "if you will accept the commission I offer, I know that the day will come when Ireland's poets will sing the honor and glory of you, greatest of them all."

"I accept," said Senchan.

Perhaps he did not realize, as Marban did, what such a quest would involve. The epic was not just lost, it was *very* lost. Senchan and his followers could spend years, if not the rest of their lives, searching for it. No doubt this is exactly what Marban hoped.

And so, sixteen months after their arrival, the poets prepared to leave. On the last night of their stay, as firelight flickered on the wall, Senchan again picked up his harp and began to strum. This, his last poem, would also be in praise of King Guaire.

"We depart from thee O stainless Guaire!
We leave thee with our blessing . . ."

He went on then to tell how many of them there had been and how long they had stayed—as if Guaire hadn't noticed. They had been treated well, said Senchan, and Guaire's hospitable heart must have warmed to know they felt that way.

But what Guaire the Hospitable felt when he heard the last three lines of Senchan's poem we can only imagine.

". . . should we return to our own land,
we shall visit thee again, O Guaire,
though now we depart."

Talk about It

- Think of someone whose home you especially like to visit. What does that person do to help you have a good time? What do you do to help your guests have a good time?

- Try to imagine how you would act if you honestly saw each guest in your home and each stranger you met as Christ. If possible, hold a dinner party or a barbecue or another type of get-together for friends of your family and try to think of them as Christ while they're in your home. Afterward, as a family, talk about what happened and how you felt.

Prayer

Give me a hospitable heart, Lord. Let me care more
for the comfort of others than for my own comfort.
Let me see you in the people around me and treat
them as I would treat you.
Lord, give me a hospitable heart.
Amen.

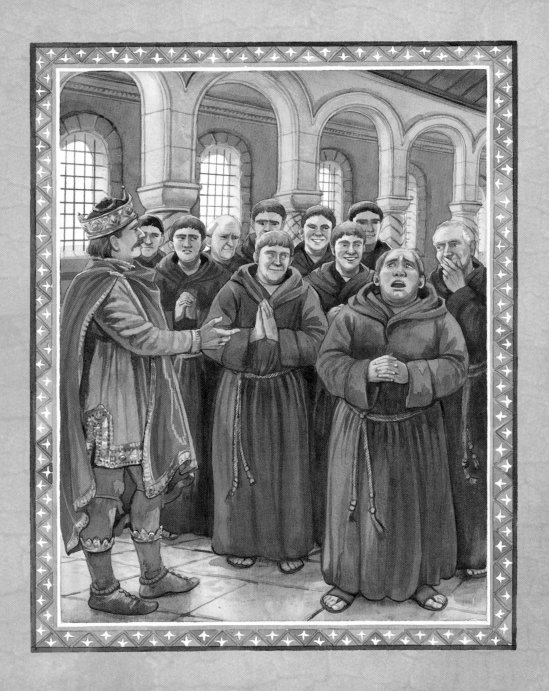

The Emperor and a Grubby Little Churchman

CHARLEMAGNE OF THE FRANKS
A.D. 742–814

Charlemagne (shar-luh-MAIN; in English, Charles the Great) inherited half his kingdom when his father, Pepin the Short, died in 768. Charlemagne inherited the other half when his brother, Carloman, died in 771. It was a huge kingdom. Charlemagne promptly made it larger, too, through wars with his various neighbors. Eventually the pope crowned him emperor.

Charlemagne loved learning and established many schools. He could speak Old Teutonic and Latin and he understood some Greek. But strangely, even though he could read, he never learned to write.

Charlemagne also loved Christ and made his faith a part of his life. He considered himself in charge of the church in his empire and could quote the Bible better than many of the clergy. He had a special love for poor and lowly people, and he taxed rich people to help the less fortunate. Furthermore, he cared about liturgy and church music and went to a great deal of trouble to ensure that it was done properly in the churches. Sometimes Charlemagne's love for church music led him to make wise decisions. Occasionally it just made him angry.

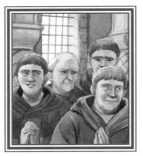

ONE DAY, during a festival church service, Charlemagne happened to be standing next to a bishop. As part of the service, a young relative of the emperor sang an "Alleluia" and did a beautiful job of it.

"That young man of ours certainly sang well!" said Charlemagne to the bishop.

But the bishop had a tin ear. He didn't realize how well the young man had sung. Furthermore, he didn't know the young man. He thought he was a nobody, and the bishop had no time for nobodies.

So he curled his fine lip and drawled, "Oh, yes. That's just how the country bumpkins drone when they're out following the oxen that pull the plow."

Charlemagne glared at the bishop. He didn't call him a witless nincompoop. He didn't waste any words on him at all. He just knocked him flat to the ground.

Another time Charlemagne was on a journey and visited a great cathedral while the worship service was going on.

At the same time, a poor, wandering monk came to the same cathedral. He didn't realize that the emperor, who was an expert on church music, was there. He just noticed that all the other monks seemed to be standing together in that section of the cathedral called the choir, and he went over to join them.

All of a sudden, the monks began to chant. The poor wanderer jumped as if he'd been shot. What they were doing was glorious! But he couldn't do it. He'd never learned how. So he just stood there, his face hot and red, like an idiot.

Then, to make matters worse, the choirmaster noticed him and moved in his direction.

"If you do not open your mouth and sing," hissed the choirmaster, raising his baton, "I am going to hit you."

Now the poor wandering monk didn't know what to do. Somehow the other monks had pressed all around him so he couldn't sneak away. And he certainly didn't want to be hit. So he opened his mouth as wide as he could, waggled his bottom jaw up and down, and tried to look like someone singing.

It was too much for many in the congregation. They burst out laughing. The more they laughed, the more the poor monk tried to look like he *was* singing. That made them laugh harder.

Not Charlemagne, though. He sat peacefully until the service was over. Then he called to the monk.

By now the monk realized who this was. Fervently he prayed that a hole would suddenly appear in the cathedral floor so he could throw himself into it.

"Your—Your Mightiness!" he croaked and crashed to his knees before Charlemagne.

He was too mortified to see the smile in Charlemagne's eyes. But he could hear the kindness in his voice as the emperor said, "My good monk, I just wanted to thank you for, uh, all your efforts at singing."

Then the monk smiled, too, and his smile grew even broader when Charlemagne ordered his men to give the monk a pound of silver so he should not be so poor.

At one time there lived at Charlemagne's court a humble little churchman, whom people considered to be barely a priest. He was rather grubby and slow and not very good at his studies. Everyone else thought Charlemagne should send him away.

"He's useless!" they all said. "He can't do anything right."

But Charlemagne felt sorry for the poor fellow and refused to send him away.

Then one day a messenger arrived to tell Charlemagne that one of the bishops had died. As head of the church, Charlemagne had to choose a new bishop to take the dead man's place.

He thought for a while and then sent for one of his church-men who was known to be well educated and capable.

"You," said Charlemagne, "shall be the new bishop."

The man was thrilled. He was more than thrilled. He was *wild* with joy. At once he prepared a huge feast at his home and invited all of the important people he knew. Needless to say, he didn't invite the grubby little churchman.

Now it just happened that the day of his feast was also Saint Martin's Eve, a special day in the church. An evening worship ser-vice was to be held, and earlier in the day the choirmaster had assigned to each choir member the phrase he was to chant all alone.

One of those singers was the churchman who was to become a bishop. But he hadn't yet heard his good news at the rehearsal. And after he did hear it, he forgot that things like rehearsals even existed.

In fact, by the time of the church service, that bishop-to-be had probably forgotten his own name. Stuffed with food, drunk with wine, and almost asleep, all he could mutter was, 'Gran' day. 'Gran' day, indeed!" Needless to say, he did not show up at the church service.

Since he had always seemed to be a well-educated, capable churchman, the others at the service just assumed he was there. They didn't even miss him until it was time for him to chant his part. Then—silence.

Everyone looked around. Where could he be? What should they do? Then they began to poke one another.

"You chant it."

"No, you."

"Not me! It's not my job to chant someone else's part."

"Come now, *one* of you must chant it!" thundered a voice.

It was Charlemagne.

Now everyone was scared and dry-mouthed, everyone except

one small, humble, grubby churchman. The emperor's voice had touched something deep inside him.

"Dear God," he prayed silently, "I do believe it is your will that *I* chant that part. Oh, dear God, help me!"

And with that, he opened his mouth and began to chant. It was ghastly. The poor man didn't know the part at all. His shaky little voice wandered all over the place and his eyes filled with panic.

"Bless his heart, he'll never make it through," thought Charlemagne. He barked, "You others! Help him out!"

The other singers obeyed promptly this time, but the grubby little churchman was so lost by then that he couldn't find the melody even when it was thundering in his ears.

Then, when his part should have ended, he kept going and chanted the first part of the Lord's Prayer. And as he did that, his voice suddenly grew strong and carried the melody like a perfect golden thread.

"Stop him!" muttered the other singers. "This isn't the right place in the service for the Lord's Prayer. He's making a mess of everything."

"No," ordered Charlemagne. "Let him sing."

"Thy kingdom come," chanted the grubby little churchman.

"Thy will be done," chanted the others.

And then it was over.

The grubby little churchman crept from the church, hoping that he would never have to see another human being again. He didn't quite cry himself to sleep. But he came close to it.

Then, early the next morning, a servant came for him.

"You are to go to the emperor in his bedchamber," said the servant.

"What?" squeaked the grubby little churchman. "Why?"

"I don't know," said the servant. "But I can guess. Everyone has heard about that church service."

"Dear God, help me!" prayed the grubby little churchman. He shook all the way to Charlemagne's bedchamber.

"Who told you to sing that part?" asked Charlemagne.

The grubby little churchman's tongue felt like shredded cabbage, but he stammered out, "My lord, you said someone must sing."

"But then why did you go on with the Lord's Prayer?"

"Blessed sire, beneficent emperor," said the grubby little churchman—he'd heard those fine words somewhere—"when I couldn't find the melody for that part, I was afraid I would displease you. So I went on with something I knew."

Charlemagne smiled gently at the frightened little fellow then took him before all the nobles.

"A certain proud man, whom I just appointed bishop, apparently has no respect or honor for me or for God. He couldn't put off his party even long enough to chant the music assigned to him. Therefore, he shall not be the new bishop."

Charlemagne turned to the grubby little churchman. "You shall be the new bishop instead. That is what God wants and what I want. Now, try to do a good job."

The grubby little churchman beamed: "I will."

Charlemagne died in 814 at the age of seventy-two. He had ruled his immense empire for almost forty-seven years. Many scholars believe that he shaped the history of Western Europe for hundreds of years to come, especially by all he did in the church. But with all Charlemagne's great deeds, it just might be that he pleased God even more when he stopped to help someone poor, frightened, or grubby.

Talk about It

- Talk about a time when you felt a bit like the grubby little churchman—frightened or alone or embarrassed. Did anyone help you? What happened?

- Describe some person you know who is like the grubby little churchman, someone other people make fun of or ignore. Think of one small, kind thing you could do for that person (whom God loves just as much as anyone else). Then do it.

Prayer

Sing or say together this second verse from the Christmas song, "Once in Royal David's City."

"He came down to earth from heaven,
who is God and Lord of all,
and his shelter was a stable,
and his cradle was a stall;
with the poor, the scorned, the lowly,
lived on earth our Savior holy."
—CECIL FRANCES ALEXANDER

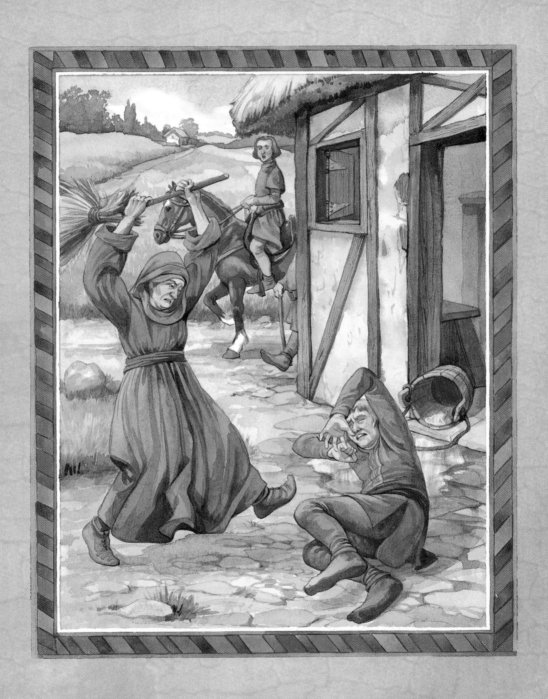

The King Who Was Beaten with a Broom

ALFRED THE GREAT OF WESSEX
A.D. 849–901

ack in the ninth century, England was divided into small king-doms, each with its own ruler. One of these kingdoms in the south was Wessex, and its ruler was King Ethelwulf (ETH-el-woolf). Ethelwulf and his wife, Queen Osburga (ahs-BUR-guh), had six children, but from the start, they knew there was something special about the fourth one, Alfred.

When he was only four, they sent him to stay with Pope Leo IV in Rome for a while. When he was six, his father took him to Rome again. So Alfred grew up deeply religious. But he was deeply troubled, too. His health was never good. Worse, though, Alfred worried that he wasn't good enough, that he had too many shortcomings.

The world around Alfred wasn't especially cheerful either. Danish invaders continually attacked the English kingdoms, burning, looting, and killing. By the time Alfred was twenty-two, his father and all his older broth-ers were dead, and he was crowned king of Wessex.

Alfred had an idea of what a good life his people could lead. But the idea would never come true while the Danes still threatened. So Alfred, like his father and brothers before him, went on fighting them—sometimes success-fully, but more often not. And then came Christmas of 878.

ALFRED AND HIS SOLDIERS were at a place called Chippenham, just about to enjoy a Christmas banquet.

"Thank heaven there are these times of rest between battles," thought Alfred. "At least the killing has stopped long enough for us to celebrate the birth of our Lord in peace."

Then he heard them—shouts outside, soon followed by the clanking of sword against sword. The Danes were attacking again.

"To your weapons, men!" he cried as he leaped to his feet. In a moment, they had all dashed out the door, their uneaten dinner forgotten.

Valiantly they tried to cut their way through the Danes. But the enemy, as organized and as fierce as ever, used their benefit of surprise to the fullest. They killed many of Alfred's soldiers, and Alfred himself barely managed to escape with a few followers.

Swiftly they fled until they reached the swamps at Athelney. There they made little boats of branches and animal skins and tied bundles of rushes into crude rafts. Silently they sailed through the swamps until they reached solid ground in the center. Only then did they build a camp and rest.

"Are we really safe here?" wondered Alfred. He soon learned that they were not. The Danes wanted England—all of England—and they knew they would never get it until they'd killed Alfred. So they continued their relentless hunt, and Alfred and his men had to flee again and again.

Sometimes they disguised themselves so the Danes wouldn't recognize them. Once while Alfred was disguised as a poor peasant, an event occurred that eventually grew into a legend.

At the time, he had separated himself from his men and was wandering from place to place. One day he came upon a hut, set off by itself in the marshes. Alfred felt tired and hoped he could rest at the hut for a while. So he knocked on the door. A peasant woman, wife of a cowherd, opened it.

"Yes?"

"I have been traveling a long, weary way, my good woman, and feel the need for rest," said Alfred. "Might I stay here for a bit?"

"You poor fellow," said the woman. "You do look worn. Come in and sit by the fire."

"Thank you," said Alfred. "You are very kind." And he sat down by the fire.

"I imagine some fresh well water might taste good to you, too," said the woman.

Alfred nodded. "Yes, it would."

"I'll go fetch some then," she said. "But see? I am just now baking some loaves. Very soon they will need to be turned. Pray, watch them and turn them when it's time so they don't burn."

"Of course," said Alfred.

"Burn," he thought. "Just the word makes me think about the Danes burning and killing their way across my land. How often has one of my men come home to find his family slain and all he owns reduced to a heap of ashes. There *must* be a way to stop them. If I can just get enough men together and catch them at the proper— What on earth is that smell?"

"My loaves!" shrieked the woman from the doorway. She dropped her bucket of water on the floor and rushed to the fire. "They're scorched! No, they're burned to a crisp. You stupid oaf, couldn't you even watch a few loaves? Do you think I'm a rich woman that I can afford to let my food go up in smoke? Well, let's see how you like this! And this!"

She beat Alfred with her broom until she'd driven him out of the hut. Then she beat him some more.

"Umph! Ouch! I'm sorry, my good woman. Truly I am!" cried Alfred.

Just them some of Alfred's followers arrived and, dismounting from their horses, knelt on one knee before him.

"Your Majesty," they each said.

"Majesty?" The woman's mouth fell open and she turned pale. "Who are you then? Surely you aren't—oh, dear Lord, preserve me!"

She fell down on both knees before Alfred and begged for forgiveness as the tears streamed down her face.

"Stop crying," said Alfred gently, "and for heaven's sake, get up. I said I'd watch your loaves and I didn't do it. You had every right to be angry with me. Now let there be peace between us."

This story may or may not be true in all its details. Legends often tell us more of how people felt about someone than they do about historical facts. In that case, the tale of Alfred and the peasant woman tells us that people thought Alfred was an extremely fair and just king.

Running from place to place in those swamps like a hunted animal, Alfred must have sometimes felt about as dejected as anyone could feel. But the strong faith in God he had shown as a little boy did not leave him when he was a man. Years after his ordeal in the swamps, he wrote, "The soul made fast to God is like a ship riding securely on her anchor." He also wrote, "I say, as do all Christian men, that it is the divine purpose that rules, not fate."

Perhaps he felt that divine purpose at work as more and more men gathered to follow him. Soon there were hundreds of them, enough to form an army and march against the Danes.

"First, though," he told himself, "I must find out what is going on with the Danes. I have had enough of their surprises. This time I want to be prepared. I want to know how many of them there are, what sort of weapons they have, and anything else that can be learned about them. And the way to find out is to send a spy into their camp."

Alfred looked at his men. "It will be a very dangerous job," he thought. "If the Danes catch a spy, they will make sure he suffers a horrible death. I cannot possibly ask one of my men to do it. So, I will do it myself."

Fortunately, Alfred could play the harp and sing. So he disguised himself as a wandering minstrel—singer of tales and poems—and made his way to the Danish camp.

"I have come to entertain you," he announced boldly.

"Wonderful!" replied the Danes. "We could do with some songs."

So Alfred played and sang for them. The Danes thought he was a fine minstrel and asked him to play and sing some more. Everyone had a great time. But while Alfred was playing and singing, he was also noticing with all his might. Soon he had a good idea of how many Danish soldiers there were as well as the sort of weapons they used. And when he had heard all he needed to know, he stood up to leave.

"Just a moment," said Guthrum, the Danish leader.

Alfred's heart might have sunk at these words, but he smiled a broad smile and faced Guthrum.

"Yes, my lord?"

"You have given us such pleasure," said Guthrum. "You must allow me to give you something in return." And he handed Alfred a sack of money.

We can be sure that Alfred didn't start laughing until he was well away from the Danish camp.

At last the time came when he could lead his army against the Danes. They met the enemy at a place called Edington, and from the first moment, Alfred's men fought every bit as fiercely as Guthrum's.

Now it happened that the Danes had a large banner with a great black raven embroidered on it. They firmly believed that this banner brought them good luck, and they carried it into every battle. But early in the battle at Edington, the English captured the banner. The Danes were appalled.

"How can we hope to win without our raven banner?" they asked one another. "Surely we all will be massacred!"

So deep was their superstition about the banner that they threw down their weapons and surrendered to Alfred and his men. Now it was up to Alfred to work out the terms of a peace treaty.

"We shall divide England between us," he declared to Guthrum. "You shall rule in the north and I in the south."

"That is agreeable with me," said Guthrum.

"Furthermore," continued Alfred, "you and all of your men will be baptized and become Christians."

"That too is agreeable," said Guthrum.

"And you will change your name," Alfred told him. "Guthrum is a heathen name. After your baptism, you will be known as Athelstan."

Guthrum bowed his head. "Thank you," he said.

So a huge baptismal service took place near Altheney, and for a time—a short time—England lived in peace.

A thelstan kept the terms of the treaty, but soon other Danes attacked England. Alfred reorganized the army, found better ways of defense, and built ships that became the ancestors of the royal navy. He also worked toward his vision of a better land by setting up schools and monasteries, translating books into the language of the people, improving the judicial system, encouraging explorers, and beginning a written record of the history of England. For all these reasons and more, he became known as Alfred the Great, "the most glorious of English kings."

Talk about It

- Alfred suffered from poor health and a poor self-image all his life. How do you suppose God used these things to make him the great man he was?

- Tell about a time when you have felt "the divine purpose" (God's will) helping in your life.

Prayer

The first book Alfred translated into the language of his people was the book of Psalms from the Bible. Let each family member choose a favorite psalm to read aloud as a prayer.

A Prince's Choice

VLADIMIR OF RUSSIA
A.D. 955–1015

*T*he wandering tribes of Slavs who settled along the waterways of what is now Russia could have had an easy time of it. Their lands were rich in natural resources, and they traded for what they didn't have. But they simply could not get along and spent much of their time in tribal warfare.

In the ninth century, Swedish chieftains came to rule over them (some say the desperate Slavs invited them), and the scattered tribes became known as the land of Rus (ROOS). The greatest chieftain was a man called Rurik (ROO-reek), and he established his capital at Kiev (key-EV), which grew into an important and beautiful city with ties to the powerful Byzantine empire and Western Europe.

But fighting and bloodshed continued. When Sviatoslav (svee-AH-toh-slahv) became prince of Kiev, he battled any number of tribes. Finally, one of them killed him, covered his skull with gold, and turned it into a drinking cup. It was not a gentle era.

Vladimir (VLAH-dee-meer), one of Sviatoslav's sons, murdered his older brother and became prince of Kiev. Vladimir fought his share of wars, too. But he also took a moment to sniff the air around him. Change was in the wind, and Vladimir thought perhaps he'd better pay attention.

"PEOPLE ARE PUTTING ASIDE the old ways of belief," he thought. "'Pagan' they call them now. The spirits of nature are no longer important. Why, in just the last twenty-five years, Rome has worked her spell on Poland, Denmark, Norway, and Hungary—turned them all into Christians. Well, if there's one thing we can take pride in, it's that no Roman sandal has ever touched the soil of Rus. Too far for them—or maybe too fierce. They didn't leave any of their fancy roads or buildings behind here. None of their fancy ideas either."

He concentrated for a moment on picking a piece of meat from between his teeth with his thumbnail. But he couldn't keep his thoughts away from his neighbors and the way their religions seemed to consume them.

"Of course the Khazar (KAH-zahr) tribe has been Jewish for at least a hundred years. Even when my father took their best fortress, sacked their capital city, and smashed their power to bits, they still hung on to their Jewishness. Then there are the Volga (VUHL-guh) Bulgars. It hasn't been that long since they chose Islam, and they're still as happy with it as a kid with a new toy."

He scratched his head and flicked a louse onto the floor.

"Maybe it's time we put aside the old ways, too. Personally, I can't see that they've ever done much for us. Just a bunch of superstitions really, and no two tribes ever see them in quite the same way. Gives them something else to fight about—as if they needed it. No, I think maybe I ought to look into these other religions, see which one seems best for us."

He clapped his hands and shouted, and one of his underlings rushed into the room.

"Yes, sir?"

"I want to hold some meetings," said Vladimir. "I want

representatives from each of the major religions to come see me. You know: the Jews, the Muslims, and the Christians in Rome. Oh yes, and the Greeks, too. I think their Christianity is different from that of Rome. I want all these representatives to tell me about what they believe. Then maybe I'll decide which religion—if any—is best for Rus."

It wasn't long before the representatives began to arrive. First came the Bulgar, whose people now followed Islam.

"Well, sir," he said, "we do believe in God."

Vladimir nodded. "I thought you did. What else?"

"We believe that Mahomet was God's prophet who told us what we should and shouldn't do."

"Such as?" Vladimir looked suspicious. He didn't like anyone telling him what he should and shouldn't do.

"Well, all men must be circumcised. And no one should eat pork or drink wine. After we die, we will have a marvelous time and all our desires will be fulfilled. But until then . . ."

"No pork?" thundered Vladimir. "No wine? But drinking is our greatest joy! We wouldn't survive without our wine. I'm afraid Islam would not work for us at all."

Next came several representatives whom the pope had sent from Rome.

"Each person fasts as much or as little as he or she can," they explained. "It's all a matter of personal strength. But when we do eat or drink something, we do it to the glory of God. That is what our teacher Paul said to us about such things."

"At least they don't forbid wine," thought Vladimir. But there was something about their words—or them—that bothered him. He couldn't put his finger on it, but . . .

"No, no, go away," he said. "Our ancestors didn't do this kind of fasting and eating thing and neither will we." His answer made no sense, but he didn't care.

The Khazars told him that Jewish law required circumcision and prohibited the eating of pork, too.

"You must also understand," they continued, "that Jerusalem is our real home. But God became angry with our ancestors and scattered us all over among the Gentiles."

"Well then," sneered Vladimir, "how can you expect anyone else to want to join you? If your own God did this to you, he mustn't think much of you. Why would we want to share your fate?"

"But, sir," began the Jewish representatives. Vladimir refused to listen.

"Go now," he ordered. "My people and I do not want to be Jews."

Finally, the Greeks arrived to tell about the Orthodox Christian church. They had prepared quite a presentation, beginning with God's creation of the world. As they moved through history, they managed to say something a bit nasty about each of the other religions. But that was not what troubled Vladimir.

"I simply do not understand," he said, "why God sent his Son, Jesus, to earth and why he let Jesus suffer and die."

"But, sir, it was for our salvation!" replied the Greeks. "God let Jesus die so that we might live and be his own dear children forever."

Vladimir shook his head. "I would never do such a thing," he said. "Why should God? No, I do not understand it."

In the days that followed, Vladimir thought some more about what the representatives had said. For a while he was afraid he'd never be able to make up his mind. But then he had an idea.

"I will send people to visit the various places of worship," he announced. "They will go to the temples of the Bulgars and the churches of the Roman and the Greek Christians. They need not visit the Jews, because I think I would find it too hard to be a

Jew. But when they've been to all these places, they will come back and tell me what they have seen with their own eyes. Perhaps then I shall be able to decide."

So the emissaries set out, and Vladimir waited impatiently for their return.

"Tell me!" he demanded when the weary travelers stumbled home at last.

"First, sir," they said, "we visited the mosques, the temples of the Bulgars."

"And?"

"They were quite plain and uncomfortable, sir. Their religion is not for us."

"I see," smiled Vladimir, thinking of the wine he would not have to give up. "Then what?"

"Then we went to the churches of the Roman Christians. They were, well, all right. But we beheld no glory there."

Vladimir nodded. "And the Greeks?"

The faces of the emissaries lit up.

"Ah, the Greeks!" they cried. "They took us to the churches where they worship their God and, oh, sir!—we hardly knew if we were in heaven or on earth. We have never before seen such beauty and such splendor—not on this earth. We have discussed among ourselves how we might describe it to you. But the truth is, sir, that it is beyond description. The worship service is incredibly lovely, sir. And we all felt it, we truly did—in those churches God dwells among his people."

"But—" Vladimir frowned. "But that is like what they told me, that God sent his Son to dwell on earth. If that is so, and if he died and rose again, surely he would not return to this sad place."

"If you had been with us, sir," said the emissaries, "you would know that he is here."

Then Vladimir retired to be alone with his thoughts. If it were true that God was still with his people, right here, right now, life would be a very different thing. Harder in some ways, but also much more glorious. Could he choose that for himself, for his people?

Politically it would be a wise choice. It would give him ties with the powerful Byzantine emperor. But would his wild, almost primitive people be able to accept such a different way of life? Would he?

And then Vladimir remembered someone he had not thought of in a long time—his grandmother Olga. She too had been a pagan, married to a pagan prince. When her husband was murdered, she saw to it that his assassins were scalded to death and their friends butchered as well.

But when Olga was an old woman, she embraced the Orthodox faith with her whole heart. She was baptized and even tried to bring Christian missionaries to Rus.

That didn't work. Olga could not even persuade her own son, Vladimir's father, to accept the Christian faith. But now her memory shone bright in the mind of her grandson. It was almost as if she said, "You, Vladimir. You are the one whom God will use to answer my prayers. You will bring Christ to my people."

And Vladimir knew she was right.

Vladimir was baptized into the Christian faith around 989 and forced his people to become Christians, too. (These were not gentle times.) He also married Anna, sister of the Byzantine emperor, and took his new faith more seriously each day. Eventually his generosity to the poor, mercy to the criminals, and support of missionaries proclaimed him a changed man and caused both him and his grandmother Olga to be recognized as saints.

Talk about It

- Imagine that you are a representative of your faith, standing before Vladimir. You probably have time to speak only a few sentences. What would you say?

- It was the memory of Vladimir's grandmother that finally made up his mind. Share memories of your older relatives and what they have meant to you.

Prayer

Thank you, Lord Christ, for all those people
who have gone before and passed their faith on to us.
Help us to pass our faith on to others in ways
that will show them that your love for all people
is real and forever.
Amen.

Too Good to Be King

EDWARD THE CONFESSOR OF ENGLAND
A.D. 1004–1066

ngland's problems with Danish invaders did not go away after the reign of Alfred the Great. England was a rich land, and the Danes wanted those riches. King Ethelred bought off the invaders for as long as he could, but by 1014, King Swein (SVANE) of Denmark had taken over the whole country. Then he died and, after a period of confusion, his son Cnut (kuh-NOOT) took England's throne.

Gentleness was not one of Cnut's virtues. He ruled by fear and slaughtered anyone who got in his way. At the same time, he generously supported the church and considered himself a full-fledged Christian. His enemies respected him, and so he was able to hold England together until his death.

Cnut's son, Harthacnut (HAHR-tuh-kuh-noot), must have had a premonition that he wouldn't live long, because he named his heir before he was even twenty-four. He chose someone to whom he wasn't even related: Edward, son of Ethelred and direct descendent of Alfred the Great. No one could dispute Edward's claim to the throne, even though he had lived in France for purposes of safety since he was ten years old. Harthacnut sent for him in 1041, and when the king died, very drunk at a wedding banquet in 1042, Edward was ready to wear the crown.

BUT WHO WAS EDWARD? It's hard to get to know anyone from a distance of almost a thousand years. And the people who have tried to know Edward have come up with some wildly differing pictures.

Just a spoiled rich kid, say some historians. He grew up in exile. He never dreamed he'd someday be king. So all he ever did was go hunting with his friends and lounge around. He wasn't even a good Christian. Hunting meant as much to him as God did. Well, yes, he did build Westminster Abbey. But that was when he was old, and it was just a hobby for him. No, Edward wasn't all that religious, and he was not all that bright either. In fact, he wasn't even much of a king. Fortunately, England survived in spite of him.

Then there are the people who felt that Edward was a spectacular king and about as close to God as any human being could get. They are the ones who rejoiced when, in 1161, Edward was recognized as a saint by the Roman Catholic Church.

"Look at how kind he was to the poor and the sick," they said. "Look at the visions and strange happenings that surrounded him. Look at the healing miracles he performed. Edward was a saint all right, and he well earned the name 'Confessor,' one whose life bears witness to Christ."

"He may have been a saint," say still others, "but that simply goes to show that saints shouldn't be kings. What did Edward ever accomplish for England? Did he fight great battles with other nations or expand England's territories? He did not. And a large number of the decisions he made weren't based on sound political principles. He made them because of spiritual insights. Now *that's* no way to rule a country."

Earl Leofric (LAY-oh-frik), Edward's good friend and advisor, had a picture of the king that no one else was privileged to see.

One day the two men were in church. During the celebration of the Eucharist, Leofric knelt behind the king, and both looked toward the altar, where the priest had lifted up the bread and wine.

Suddenly, though, Leofric no longer saw bread and wine. Instead, between the priest's raised hands he saw the figure of Jesus, who with his right hand was blessing Edward. Leofric stumbled to his feet to tell Edward what he had seen, but the king told him to remain still.

"What thou see'st I see," said Edward, "and him I honor."

After the service concluded, the two men talked about the vision.

"It gave me such a strong feeling of comfort," said Leofric.

"And me," agreed Edward. "Indeed, it was wonderfully comforting. But, my friend, do not speak of this thing to anyone else. Keep your knowledge to yourself."

Obviously Leofric did not keep that promise.

Another time, Edward was riding home from church when an old man stopped him.

"Please give this pilgrim alms in the name of Saint John the Evangelist," said the old man.

Now Edward would have given alms—a gift of money—to anyone who asked him. But a pilgrim, someone making a journey to honor God, was special. Furthermore, this pilgrim had asked in the name of Saint John the Evangelist, the author of the Fourth Gospel, who happened to be one of Edward's favorite saints. It was John, after all, who had been so close to Jesus that Jesus had entrusted his own mother to John's care. So Edward would have been more than happy to give the old man alms. Unfortunately, he had no money with him. He glanced down, though, and realized he was wearing a fine ring. He tugged it off his finger.

"Will you accept this in the name of Saint John the Evangelist?" he asked the old pilgrim.

"Gladly, sire, and may God bless you for your generosity."

Twenty-four years passed, and one day two Englishmen were making their way home from a pilgrimage to Palestine. On the way, they met a very old man.

"Greetings!" he said to them.

"Greetings!" they replied.

"And where are you bound, my brothers?"

"Ah, we are headed home now, sir, after a long journey to Palestine."

"Home, eh?" asked the very old man. "And what country do you call home?"

"Why, England, sir."

"That is good," the very old man nodded. "When you get there, I would like you to go to your king. Give him greetings in my name and thank him for the alms he gave to me long ago. I have kept it all this while, and now I should like you to return it to him."

And he handed one of the Englishmen a ring.

"Tell Edward," he added, "that in the space of six months he will leave this world and come to live with me forever."

The two Englishmen were so astonished by these words that they hardly knew what to say. Finally, one of them stammered, "C-can you tell us, sir, what is your name?"

"I am John the Evangelist," said the very old man, "and your king, Edward, is my friend. He has led a holy life, and for that I hold him dear."

The two Englishmen left the very old man then and went on their way, marveling at what had happened. When they reached England, they hurried as quickly as they could to Edward and told him everything.

"And here is the ring, sire," said one of them.

"This makes me so happy," said Edward, slipping it onto his

finger. "I cannot remember ever feeling such joy before. And now I shall prepare myself to die."

And when Edward did die, the ring was still on his finger. But even after his death, Edward's work lived on. Back when he was still a young man in France, he had made a solemn vow to God. So many bad things had happened to members of his family. If these misfortunes would come to an end, Edward prayed, he would show his thanks by making a pilgrimage to Saint Peter's tomb in Rome.

After he felt firmly settled on his throne in England, he called a meeting of his council and told them about the vow.

"Oh, sire, we don't think you should go!" responded the council. "Various factions might spring up here in England while you are gone and destroy the peace. Or foreign nations might take advantage of your absence to attack us. Besides, the situation in Italy is extremely unsettled at the moment. It wouldn't be safe for you to travel there."

"Well," said Edward, "let us see what the pope says."

On the whole, Pope Leo IX agreed with the council and devised an alternate way for Edward to fulfill his vow. "Edward," he said, "should figure up how much money he would have spent on the pilgrimage and then give that amount to poor people. He should also build or repair a monastery in England in honor of Saint Peter.

Edward found a little church dedicated to Saint Peter in a place called Thorney, not far from London. He had it pulled down and began work on an abbey that would take its place. For fifteen years the workers toiled. Edward loved to watch them from his palace window. Eventually the building would be known as the Abbey Church of Saint Peter at Westminster and, later still, Westminster Abbey. It was consecrated on December 28, 1065, but by then Edward was too ill to attend the ceremony. He died a week later and was buried in his abbey.

So who was this Edward? A spoiled rich boy who loved to give alms to the poor and support churches? A man who loved to hunt, but who attended church every morning? A king much too spiritual to be a good ruler, whose reign saw little internal conflict and much peace? A great man or a very human man? Maybe Edward was all of these things. We can't know for sure. But we do know that his life, in the eyes of his church, made him a confessor of Christ.

Talk about It

- Do you think someone can be too good a person to govern a country? Some people have said that about several kings and a president or two. Is there any way in which this might be true? Why would anyone say such a thing if it were not true?

- Pretend that it's a hundred years from now and people are trying to know *you*. Tell about an incident in your life that you would like them to know about.

Prayer

Dear Lord, please put our lives together
in such a way that people will
see your love in all we say and do.
Make us confessors of Christ
in our own time and place.
We ask this in his name.
Amen.

The Princess Who Wanted the World

MATILDA OF SCOTLAND
A.D. 1080–1118

*I*n 1066, William, Duke of Normandy in France, defeated Harold, king of England, at Hastings on the southern coast of England. Harold and all his brothers died in that battle. On Christmas Day, William was crowned king of England.

Meanwhile, at Westminster Palace, a young woman named Margaret lived with her younger brother and sister, Edgar and Christina. Edgar, Margaret knew, had a better right to be king than either Harold or William. He simply wasn't yet old enough. But that didn't mean he was safe from danger. At any moment, William might decide to get rid of him.

So Margaret got herself, Edgar, and Christina aboard a ship. She planned to move to Hungary, where they had friends. But a storm drove their ship to Scotland, and Margaret found herself facing rough King Malcolm.

She did not know what to expect. Would Malcolm throw these uninvited guests in prison? Kill them? Send them back to England?

No. Malcolm welcomed them warmly and offered them a home. Before long, he and Margaret were married. They had eight children, one of whom was a girl named Edith Matilda. Years later, when war again raged all around, young Edith was sent to England to live in safety with her aunt, the Abbess of Romsey, who was head of a large group of nuns.

EDITH LOOKED UP at the imposing building her aunt called home and shivered. It didn't look like the sort of place *she* would want as a home. Not that the Scottish castle that had been her home was a warm and cozy place. Hardly. Edith shivered again. In fact, she thought, she'd been cold for most of her life. But her mother, Queen Margaret, had done all she could to make the castle beautiful and welcoming. She'd taught her ladies to make tapestries and curtains to cover the windows and the cold stone walls. And she'd made it clear that everyone—rich and poor alike—was a welcome guest.

This abbey where the nuns lived, on the other hand, seemed all closed in on itself, as if it were shutting the world out . . .

"Edith! My dear child! My poor, dear, motherless, fatherless child!"

They were not the best words with which her aunt could have greeted her. Edith's eyes filled with tears. It had not been so long ago since her father and oldest brother had been killed on the battlefield. And when Edith's next oldest brother, Edgar, had brought their mother the news, Queen Margaret, already ill, had whispered a last prayer and died.

Edgar was king of Scotland now, but the country remained full of danger. "Which is why I'm here," thought Edith, "and I suppose my aunt is trying to be kind."

"Let me show you to your room," the abbess was saying. "I'm afraid you'll find everything here rather simple after what you've been used to."

"I don't mind a simple life," said Edith. She meant it. Keeping the everyday aspects of life simple left your mind free to concentrate on more important things. Things such as what life was all about and what role God expected you to play in it.

"That's good," nodded the abbess. "Come now, child. Follow me."

As the days and weeks passed, Edith's life settled into a quiet, untroubled routine. Regular worship services governed the shape of each day. In between came meals—with plenty of good, plain food—a little sewing, a bit of reading, a walk or two, and then bed. It was all very peaceful—and boring—thought Edith.

Then one day Edith's aunt summoned her to her parlor.

"You have been with us for a while now, child," she smiled. "Are you enjoying your stay?"

"Yes, Aunt," replied Edith dutifully. "I am having a very, uh, nice time."

"Good! And have the sisters been kind to you?"

"Very kind," said Edith. Actually she'd had little to do with the nuns, who were wholly involved in their own routine. But no one had ever spoken harshly to her, and one or two of them even smiled when she passed them in a hallway.

"Fine!" The abbess leaned forward in her big, elaborately carved chair. Edith, perched on a stool before her, thought she looked exactly like a mother hen fussing over her one chick.

"I think then, Edith, that it is time we discussed your future."

"My future? But I just assumed I'd stay on here until things quieted down in Scotland. Then I'd go home again."

"No, no, no." The abbess shook her head, still smiling. "That rough country is no place for a delicate young girl. You must sink your roots in safe soil where your soul as well as your mind and body can grow and flourish in the light of God's love."

"But where is such a place?" asked Edith, totally confused by now.

"Here!" exclaimed her aunt. From her lap she seized a nun's veil and clapped it on Edith's head. "You shall stay here with us and become a nun, my dear."

Horrified, Edith jumped to her feet and pulled off the veil.

"Oh no, Aunt! I could never do that. I feel quite certain that God does not mean for me to be a nun."

"Nonsense, child. You haven't given the idea a moment's thought, much less considered it prayerfully. And when you do, you'll realize that a permanent life here is the answer to all your problems. You will be cared for. You will be safe . . ."

Just when Edith thought she would surely explode, another nun came to the door with a message, and her aunt left the room for a few moments.

"Safe!" exclaimed Edith. "I don't want to be *safe*. I don't want to be shut away from the world. I want to be out there in the middle of life, *living*. If I had to be a nun, I'd go stark, staring *mad!*"

She threw the veil on the floor and stomped on it. Then, hearing her aunt's footsteps returning, she picked it up again and dusted it off as best she could.

"We won't discuss the matter any more today," said the abbess in a sad, patient voice that made Edith want to scream. "But I want you to promise me, child, that you will give it serious thought. And ask God's guidance, too, of course."

"I promise," Edith said through gritted teeth. Then she made her escape before saying something she'd later regret.

But Edith didn't give her aunt's idea much thought. Nor did she spend much time praying about it. She already knew, in the deepest core of her being, that she should not become a nun. It was not the life she wanted. It was not the life God wanted for her.

"I am a very religious person," she told herself. "Didn't I have the best teacher in the whole world in my own mother? Ever since I was a tiny child, she read me stories about Jesus from her Gospel book. Why, she even made a Christian out of my father—and that couldn't have been easy. I want to be like my mother, serving God out in the world by serving his people there."

Every so often, Edith's aunt would send for her and ask if she'd come to any conclusion.

"Not yet, Aunt," Edith would reply politely. "I'm still thinking and praying." She felt sure that a flat no would never satisfy the abbess. So she tried to buy time until some other solution presented itself.

Then Edith received a disturbing piece of news. A certain young man, whom she thoroughly disliked, had come to the abbey to ask for her hand in marriage.

"Oh no!" thought Edith. "What if my aunt decides to give me to him as another way of keeping me safe?"

Frantically she looked around her room. There, crumpled in a corner, lay the hated veil. Edith picked it up and arranged it on her head. Then she went to the parlor where her aunt and the young man were waiting.

"I am so sorry," said Edith, after appropriate greetings had been exchanged, "but I cannot marry anyone. You see, I may be very close to becoming a nun." And she looked demurely at the floor.

An hour later, the veil was back in its corner and Edith was back to "still thinking and praying."

More time passed, and an especially nasty older man came seeking Edith's hand. Out came the veil.

"I'm so sorry," said Edith, "but you see that I am almost a nun. I could not possibly marry you." This time, she thought she saw the ghost of a twinkle in her aunt's eye.

At last came news that made Edith completely forget her faithful friend, the veil. Henry, fourth son of William the Conqueror, and now king of England in his own right, wanted to marry her! For a long time, Henry hadn't stood much chance of becoming king, and so he had indulged his love of learning. But then two of his older brothers were killed in hunting accidents. Before the third brother could return from a long trip abroad, Henry had seized the throne for himself. Known as "the Good Scholar," he wanted a well-educated queen to rule beside him, and he'd settled on her—Edith.

But her aunt insisted on a private talk with her before giving Henry a final answer.

"Do you realize, child," she asked, "what you are letting yourself in for? War and politics stop here at the abbey door. As Henry's queen, you'll be thrust in the midst of them. And you don't even know if you love him—or if he loves you."

"Love isn't the first thing a princess—or a king—can think of," replied Edith. "Duty must come first. Henry must defend his throne against his brother. With my brother ruling Scotland, he knows at least one border will be safe. Furthermore, my family's heritage will make his right to the throne seem all the stronger. After all, we're descended from Alfred the Great.

"We may come to love one another or we may not. But we'll respect one another. And I'll be where God wants me to be—out there in the world where I can serve God's people."

The twinkle in the abbess's eye was unmistakable now. "Edith, I give up," she said. "Marry your king and go out into the world. And may God go with you."

"Don't worry," said Edith. "He will."

After Edith married Henry I in 1100, she used her middle name, Matilda. But the people of England soon chose their own name for her, Good Queen Maud.

Queen Matilda supported many convents and monasteries and often served poor people with her own hands. At times she even washed and kissed the feet of beggars, which utterly disgusted her royal courtiers.

"For Godde's love, Your Majesty," they would cry, "desist!"

And no doubt Good Queen Maud replied, "It is for Godde's love that I do it."

Talk about It

- If you had been in Edith's position, would you rather have married someone you didn't know or stayed safe and secure in the abbey? What other alternatives might you have looked for?

- Have family members list five things they really enjoy doing. Then have them put a star beside the things they think they do well. (It might be all five.) Talk about ways these things are—or could be—used to help God's people in God's world.

Prayer

Dear Lord, help us to understand ourselves
well enough that we know the ways
we can best serve you by helping others.
Guide and strengthen each of us in our ministries
and let them be to your glory and not our own.
Amen.

Flowers in the Snow

ELIZABETH OF HUNGARY
A.D. 1207–1231

From different directions they came, six of the best minne-singers (MINN-eh-sing-ers, *traveling poets and singers*) in the world. Through the little town of Eisenach (EYE-seh-nahk) they clattered up the 1,200-foot hill at whose summit sat the great fortress known as the Wartburg. They came to a contest of minnesingers, held by their host, Herman I of Thuringia (thuh-RIHN-jee-uh), and a very serious contest it was—since the loser would have his head chopped off.

Five minnesingers sang the praises of Herman. The sixth, Henrich von Ofterdingen, praised his own homeland, Austria, and the duke who reigned there. That displeased everyone else. Even though he was the best, it was decided that Heinrich must lose. But Heinrich thought of a way out of his dilemma. He got permission to go to Hungary and bring back Klingsor, the greatest minnesinger of all time, who would make the final judgment.

Klingsor, who was also a magician, wafted himself and Heinrich through the air and back to Thuringia on a leather blanket. Then he settled the contest so that Heinrich kept his head. Finally, Klingsor delivered a special message for Thuringia: "In Hungary a daughter is born to Queen Gertrude and King Andrew. This child, Elizabeth, will marry Ludwig of Thuringia and will one day become a saint."

Elizabeth had heard the story many times and rightly so, since it determined the course of her entire life. ("Though I'm not so sure about that flying blanket," she always told herself. "Would God really allow that sort of magic in a Christian land?")

Herman, the much-praised prince of Thuringia had liked Klingsor's words very much. He wouldn't mind an alliance with Hungary one bit. It would make Thuringia stronger and his own family more important. So he had put out feelers to see how Andrew II of Hungary felt. Andrew, licking his lips at the promise of access to Thuringia's riches, had acknowledged that he liked the idea, too.

"And that," said Elizabeth to one of her maids, "is why at the age of four I was whisked from my home and deposited here at the Wartburg to grow up with my future husband. But you know all that, of course, since you came with me from Hungary. Still, it is a good story. Except maybe for the part about the blanket."

"Just like a legend," agreed the maid. "I imagine folks will go on telling it for ages to come. I've often wondered, though, how you, a tiny child, felt when you looked up the hill at this great fortress and realized that from then on, it would be your home."

"I don't think I really understood that," mused Elizabeth, "just as I didn't understand that I'd never see my mother again or that my father would forget all about me. I simply accepted things as they came, the way a small child does. And I knew that God would take care of me, no matter what."

"You always were a religious child," said the maid. "But, tell me, what started you thinking about all these things now?"

"I don't know," replied Elizabeth. "Boredom maybe. A princess has to spend so much time just sitting around. I hate that. There are so many things I'd like to be doing."

"Such as caring for those poor folk?" suggested the maid.

"Exactly!" said Elizabeth. "It's my greatest joy, as you well know. It's God's will, too. Why does it get me in so much trouble?"

"It didn't used to get you in trouble when you were a child," observed the maid.

"No. No, it didn't. Not when Prince Herman was alive. He gave me lots of money, and said I could spend it any way I liked. Well, what I liked was to buy food and clothes for the poor people down in Eisenach. I especially liked to take food down to the hungry children. The happiness I saw on their faces when they'd had enough to eat or finally felt warm—why, that was better than anything I could buy myself. And, besides, it was doing God's will, and that always makes me feel so—well—so full of light. I think Prince Herman understood that. He never objected when I wanted to pray either."

"You prayed far more than most children. I remember that. It's too bad Prince Herman died when you were only nine."

"Yes," Elizabeth frowned, "I hadn't realized till then how much his wife, Princess Sophia, disliked me. 'You are my future daughter-in-law,' she would say. 'Please try to act like it.' Or, 'All this nonsense with the poor, Elizabeth. Don't you know that everyone is laughing at you? They think you are a little mad.' And soon people *were* laughing at me. They did it just to please her."

"But Ludwig didn't laugh at you." The maid smiled. "I think he loved you from the first moment he saw you, when you were four and he was eleven."

"I certainly loved him." Elizabeth smiled, too. "He was always so kind, so gentle. But do you know there was a time when I wasn't positive that he loved me. He was gone so much of the time. Oh, I know he had to be—it was affairs of state that took him. But I kept wondering if his mother's dislike of me hadn't affected him, too, if maybe he was laughing at me."

"And then he spoke those words to one of his knights," said the maid, "and somehow they got to me and I told them to you."

"I'll never forget those words," said Elizabeth. "Ludwig said he wouldn't desert me for a whole mountain of gold. I don't think I've ever been happier in my life—unless it was my wedding day."

Elizabeth laughed, then stood up. "I'm sorry, but I simply cannot sit here anymore. All day I've been smelling that lovely aroma of baking bread from the kitchen, and I can't help thinking of people in Eisenach who desperately need some bread."

"But you have already fed that huge crowd from the town that gathers at the gates of the fortress each day," said the maid. "Surely there can't be many hungry people left in Eisenach."

"Oh, but there are!" replied Elizabeth. "There are always hungry people left. And right now I am thinking of those who are too old or too ill to climb all the way up to the gates."

"Well, it's quite cold today," said the maid. "You had better wear your warm cloak."

"Oh, I intend to wear my cloak," smiled Elizabeth. "And you wear yours, too. I have plans for those cloaks."

"What about Ludwig's mother? What if she sees you?"

"Don't worry about Ludwig's mother. She won't see me. I know ways through this fortress that she has never dreamed of."

Elizabeth opened the door to her chamber and checked the hallway in both directions.

"No one's around," she whispered. "Now follow me as quietly as you can."

Through one doorway after another she slipped, up one staircase and down another. Finally, when the poor maid thought that surely they must end up exactly where they started, Elizabeth tugged open a last door and they found themselves in one of the kitchens. And there on a large wooden table sat row after row of loaves of freshly baked bread.

"Ah!" said Elizabeth. "Just what I need."

"But, madame," protested one of the bakers, "the Princess Sophia has said . . ."

"Quiet!" snapped the maid. "You forget yourself. Madame is princess now, and if she wishes to take bread from the kitchen of *her* fortress, it is certainly no concern of yours. Simply bake some more. Here, madame."

And she began handing loaf after loaf to Elizabeth, who clutched them under her cloak until her arms could hold no more.

"You take as many as you can under your cloak, too," she told the maid. Then the two of them set off down the road that led from the fortress to the town.

"Be careful," warned the maid. "The snow makes the road slippery. And it's hard to keep your balance with both arms tucked tightly under your cloak."

"I know," agreed Elizabeth. "But this way if—if anyone should look out of a window of the fortress, they'll just think we're taking a walk." She glanced at the maid. "You were so brave with that baker. I could never have spoken to him like that."

The maid shrugged. "He is a baker. I am maid to Princess Elizabeth. He knows his place. And I must say that it wouldn't do you any harm to be a little less meek. After all . . ."

"Look!" interrupted Elizabeth. "Isn't that Ludwig coming along the road toward us? Oh dear! What will we do now?"

"Do? Why you'll greet him as is proper for any wife. What's the matter? Are you afraid of him, child?"

"Of course not. I just don't think I'd like him to see the bread."

"Why not? You're doing nothing wrong."

"I know. I'm doing God's will. But I worry that maybe Ludwig's mother will get to him, that he'll laugh at me or be angry."

The maid just shook her head, then stepped aside as Ludwig pulled up his horse and leaped to the ground.

"Out for a walk on such a cold day?" he asked Elizabeth with a smile that made her heart melt.

"Aren't you going to give me your hand?" he asked her.

"Well—"

"I know!" teased Ludwig. "You're hiding something under your cloak."

Even though she knew he was teasing, Elizabeth could hear Sophia's cruel taunts echoing in her mind. Instinctively she pulled her cloak more tightly around her.

"Come now!" said Ludwig. "Surely you aren't running away with the family jewels. Let's see what you have."

With that he pulled open the cloak. And onto the snowy road tumbled a great heap of lilies and roses.

"Oh!" cried Elizabeth.

"Oh!" cried the maid.

"I don't understand," said Ludwig. "Such flowers! Where did you find them at this time of year?"

"I don't understand either," said Elizabeth as tears of pure joy filled her eyes and ran down her face. She knew that God approved of her work with the poor. "But, oh, God is good!"

*U*nfortunately, Ludwig died of bubonic plague after he and Elizabeth were married only six years. His brother, Henry, greedy for power, evicted Elizabeth and her three little children from the Wartburg in midwinter. Eventually she fell under the control of a cruel priest, Conrad, who took her children from her, beat her, and forced her to live in the direst poverty. Still Elizabeth tried to share the little she had with other poor people. One day, her health broken, she heard a bird singing that she would die in three days. That song made her very happy. Elizabeth died in 1231 at the age of twenty-three and has become one of the most beloved saints of all time.

Talk about It

- Why do you think Elizabeth was persecuted by Princess Sophia? Think about a time when you felt guilty or frightened even though you knew you were doing the right thing. What—or who—made you feel that way? What did you do? How did things turn out?

- Consider contacting a homeless shelter or some other helping group in your area to see if there is some sort of food or other donation you could deliver as a family.

Prayer

Help us understand, Lord God,
that your will has not been done until
no one suffers from hunger or cold. And help us
to do whatever we can to bring that day
closer when your will will be done.
Amen.

The Princess and the Dragon

JADWIGA OF POLAND
1374–1399

eography has never been Poland's friend. Most of the country lies on a wide green plain, right in the middle of Europe. Poland's farmers will say that the land isn't as good as it looks. They have to work hard to make a living. But that hasn't stopped Poland's neighbors from trying to grab as much of Poland as they can.

No natural boundaries protect Poland from Russia on the east and Germany on the west. As a result, the Polish people have suffered one bloody invasion after another.

In 966 Poland became a Roman Catholic country. This new religion made a tremendous difference. During their darkest hours, the Polish people have clung to their faith. It has been the glue that holds them together.

Sometimes a strong king came along to improve Poland's lot. Casimir (KAZ-uh-meer) the Great was one of those. But Casimir had no sons, so he suggested that his nephew, King Louis of Hungary, rule Poland after him. In 1370, Louis took over from Hungary and mostly ignored his new kingdom. He had no sons either, so the Poles agreed that one of his daughters should rule after Louis died. That daughter was Jadwiga (yahd-VEE-guh).

JADWIGA WAS ELEVEN YEARS OLD when she heard the news.

"Your father is dead, child. You must pack up your things and move to Poland. You are her ruler now."

How Jadwiga's head spun! Now? They expected her to move to Poland now? And rule that whole strange country?

She looked at her mother and older sister. Suddenly she realized how much she loved them. She thought about her home and all the dear, familiar things around her. She might not see any of them—home or family—ever again.

It was a dreadful moment. But Jadwiga was a royal child. She had been brought up knowing that princesses sometimes had to leave their homeland and make a new life among strangers. She was also a Christian child. With all her heart Jadwiga believed that no matter where she was, God would be with her.

One other thought kept Jadwiga's spirits up as the bustle of packing erupted around her: William. Prince William of Austria was her dearest friend. In fact, he was her husband. They had been officially married when she was five years old. Of course they hadn't lived together since then. But she loved William and he loved her. So someday . . .

At last the moment came. All her possessions were safely loaded. The nobles and servants who would accompany her were ready to go. All that remained was for Jadwiga to kiss her mother and sister good-bye and be helped into her own coach. "God help me," she prayed. "Be with them. Take care of them. And be with me."

Then the coaches rumbled away. Through the green Hungarian countryside. Into the thick, dark forests where wolves howled to one another and sunshine could not find its way to the ground. Up into the high mountains, looming like giant walls between Jadwiga and all she loved.

"William," she whispered to herself over and over again. "He won't let the mountains stop him. He is my husband, and he'll come to me. Then everything will be all right and we'll rule Poland together. Oh, dear God, please bring him to me soon!"

The journey seemed to take forever. But finally the weary princess saw the city walls of Krakow (KRAH-kow) towering ahead. Krakow, most beautiful of Poland's cities. Jadwiga had heard the minstrels sing of it and of the legend that gave it its name.

A huge rocky hill, Wawel (VAH-vul) Hill, rose above the city on the edge of the Vistula (VIS-chuh-luh) River. It was said that, way back in the mists of time, a dragon lived on that hill and periodically plunged down into the city to eat young girls. Then one day a cobbler called Krakus tricked the dragon into eating a dead ram stuffed with tar and sulphur. This tasty meal made the dragon unbearably thirsty, and he drank from the Vistula River until he exploded. Then Krakus married the local princess, and the city was named for him.

Jadwiga shivered. No dragon would pounce on her in Krakow. But what strange and frightening things did lie in the days ahead?

Then her coach swept across the moat and through the city gates. Krakow lay before her. Its houses looked like dwellings from a fairy tale, and the market square surged with people and color and pigeons. And there stood Wawel Hill with proud Wawel Castle and Wawel Cathedral standing guard at the top.

Before long, Jadwiga lost all sense of time. She felt like a doll or a puppet. Other people moved her from place to place. They bathed her and dressed her in the stiff, heavy robes of royalty. At last she found herself in the cathedral atop Wawel Hill, and a voice was proclaiming, "I now crown you king of Poland, *in nomine Patris, et Filii, et Spiritus Sancti.*"

In the name of the Father and the Son and the Holy Spirit, she—Jadwiga—was now king of Poland. King? Yes, king. It seemed that the Poles, while willing to have a woman rule them, would not stand for her being merely a queen, and so they crowned her king.

Jadwiga stood as straight and tall as she could with those heavy robes on her body, the scepter in her hand, and the crown pressing down on her head. As her new subjects looked at their king, they saw a sturdy little girl with black curls tumbling past her shoulders, huge dark eyes, and a firm chin. What sort of ruler would this child make? Well, never mind. They had already made careful plans for her future.

Of course Jadwiga still had her plans, too, and at the heart of those plans was William.

"I hope he'll be coming soon," she said almost every day. "I will be able to do a much better job of ruling Poland when William is here to rule with me."

Then one day she learned the dreadful truth.

"There is no way, Your Majesty, that the Polish people will allow an Austrian prince to rule them. Forget about William."

Forget about William? That was absurd. He was her husband. How could she forget him?

But the worst was yet to come.

"We feel, Your Majesty, that it would be in the best interests of Poland if you marry Jagiello (yah-gee-EL-lo), grand duke of our neighbor to the east, Lithuania."

Jadwiga was horrified. She'd heard the minstrels sing about Jagiello. They called him a "hairy barbarian." She'd rather be eaten by that dragon that once lived on Wawel Hill than marry Jagiello.

"I can't marry him!" she cried. "Why, Jagiello isn't even a Christian."

"That's the whole point," purred the noblemen surrounding

her. "You see, those pagan Lithuanians have been giving Poland trouble for years. But if you marry Jagiello, Lithuania will accept Christianity. Our two countries will have to stop fighting. We'll become friends. Allies. It's a heaven-sent opportunity, Your Majesty. Think about it."

Jadwiga lifted her chin and her eyes flashed. "There is nothing to think about," she declared. "I will not marry Jagiello. I love William."

Jadwiga would not change her mind and, to her delight, she soon discovered that William felt the same. Bravely he made his way into Krakow and to Jadwiga.

"We'll talk to the nobles together," he assured her. "Surely the two of us together will be able to make them see reason."

And so the two young people reasoned and then stormed and then pleaded with the Polish nobles—all to no avail.

"Poland does not want an Austrian ruler," they were told. "And we need the alliance with Jagiello."

Finally, out of patience, the Polish officials sent William packing back to Austria.

Then Jadwiga felt completely alone. And that was when the Polish clergy began talking with her.

"It is not an easy thing you are being asked to do, Your Majesty," they said. "Naturally you do not want to marry this strange man about whom you have heard so many nasty things. But it is your duty, child. You must do it for the good of Poland."

"But I am already married," said Jadwiga. "William is my husband. Surely God wouldn't want me to break my vows."

"A marriage of children," smiled the clergy. "Such a thing has no validity in the eyes of God. You and William have never even lived together as husband and wife."

"But . . ." Jadwiga's eyes filled with tears. Their voices were so soft, so persuasive. She couldn't yield. She just couldn't.

"Think, Jadwiga," the voices continued. "Think of bringing peace to two countries. Even more, think of bringing all those lost Lithuanian souls to our Lord Jesus Christ. It may not be a pleasant duty, but it is a high and holy calling, child. And it is what God wants you to do."

Jadwiga put her hands over her face. If only their words would stop fluttering around her like so many little birds, each one whispering, "You must!"

Finally, she closed her eyes and tried to hear the voice of God within herself. "You are my God who is always with me," she prayed. "You are my God who guides me, protects me, and—yes—uses me to help other people. Oh, help me know what to do!"

God must have answered her prayer, for when Jadwiga looked up and spoke, her face was calm and her voice was steady.

"I will do it," she said. "I will marry Jagiello."

The next day, Jadwiga slipped into Wawel Cathedral and knelt before a wooden cross. She spent the entire day on her knees there. When she arose, she felt the warmth of God's love surrounding her like a cloak and the assurance of God's grace burning strong in her heart. She was ready for whatever her new life might bring.

At the age of fourteen, Jadwiga married Jagiello, and they became co-kings of Poland. Jagiello accepted Christianity and promptly began bullying his fellow Lithuanians into accepting it, too. Jadwiga, meanwhile, devoted herself to living as simply as she could and to helping poor people.

From their marriage came a line of kings who ruled Poland for nearly two hundred years and brought the Polish people one of the most golden eras in their history.

Jadwiga died in childbirth at the age of twenty-five. A plaque beneath a wooden cross in Wawel Cathedral still proclaims: "Here knelt Jadwiga."

Talk about It

- Because she couldn't look into the future, Jadwiga never knew the great good her marriage did for the Polish people. Do you think her decision would have been easier if she had been able to see the future?

- Think of something nobody in your family would really want to do—even if it might help someone in need. What is keeping you from helping those people? How might it help you to pray for God's guidance?

Prayer

As a family, pray for God's good advice on how to overcome things that keep you from helping others, for sharp minds to hear that advice—and for courage to follow the advice.

"Till Death Us Do Part"

KATARINA OF SWEDEN
A.D. 1526–1583

I n the sixteenth century, Sweden was not some remote land to the north, locked away by distance and climate from the rest of Europe. Instead, the Swedish people played an important role in the lives of their neighbors—England, Denmark, Poland, and Russia—and in those of the Mediterranean countries, too.

In 1560, King Gustavus Vasa died, and his eldest son became King Erik XIV. Erik had two half brothers, John and Karl, and they became dukes. John ruled in Finland and Karl ruled in Sodermanland, both territories of Sweden. Although they could do pretty much as they liked in their own territories, in some ways they were still responsible to Erik. Unfortunately, the definition of their responsibilities was rather vague, which inevitably led to trouble, especially when John fell in love with the Polish princess, Katarina.

Actually, Katarina was only half Polish. Her father was King Sigismund (SEEG-ees-mont) I of Poland, but her mother, Bona Sforza (BOH-nah-SFORT-zah), was from Italy. Katarina spoke at least five languages. She was also exceptionally beautiful, and many men sought her hand. But John was determined to win her for himself, and that's where the trouble started.

BY THE TIME JOHN was wooing Katarina, her brother, Sigismund II, ruled Poland, and he needed money.

"I believe I have the solution to both our problems," said John. "You give me the hand of your sister in marriage, and I will lend you the money you need. We'll count it as part of the marriage settlement I would make anyway. But since it *is* a loan, you might put up some of your castles as a pledge to repay it someday."

The proposal looked good to Sigismund, too, and he agreed. So in 1562, John and Katarina were married among great festivities in Poland. Of course they invited all their relatives to the ceremony. But Erik didn't come. He was furious.

"Just who does John think he is to set up an agreement with the king of another country?" he stormed. "*I* am the king of Sweden and he's only my miserable little duke. John's going to pay for this presumptuous behavior and he's going to pay dearly!"

Meanwhile, with the wedding festivities over, John and Katarina prepared to sail to their home in Finland. They left from the port city of Riga, but they didn't get far. Soon their ship was firmly locked in ice.

"Not a very good beginning to our marriage," said John ruefully.

"Never mind," replied Katarina. "We'll get to Finland eventually, and meanwhile, we are together." She had already learned to love this determined man who so dearly loved her.

Workers cut a channel through the ice, and the ship returned to Riga. There they waited for forty weeks for the weather to improve. (It must have been a *very* cold year.)

At last, though, they sailed, and Katarina began to count the days until she would see her new home. But they had not quite reached Finland when Swedish sailors stormed their boat, took it over, and dumped the passengers on the shore.

"I suspect brother Erik had something to do with this," growled John. "Are you prepared for a long walk, my dear?"

"Of course," said Katarina.

So they walked the remaining thirty miles to Finland.

"Almost there," puffed John at last. "And wait till you see the warm welcome my Finnish people give you. There will be a delegation to sing our praises and nice warm sleighs to bear us home."

But when they reached the border, they saw no delegation at all and no nice warm sleighs either. All that greeted them was one lonely sled, big enough to hold the queen and no one else.

"This is an outrage!" shouted John. "Where are my people? Has Erik corrupted them, too?"

Word spread of the dishonor done the duke and his bride, and suddenly five hundred horsemen appeared.

"We have come to bear you home," they cried, and that is exactly what they did. Soon Katarina found herself in the royal quarters, her calendar filled with dinners and dances and other welcoming events.

"You see, John?" she said one day. "I knew it would come out all right. Now that we're safely home, we can relax and truly begin our life together."

"I'm afraid not," sighed John. "I've just had word from Erik. He is accusing me of treason. He says I have made an independent treaty with a foreign power—that's your brother, dear—and I have withheld taxes. He has released the Finnish people from their oath of faithfulness to me and is sending soldiers to take both of us to Sweden."

"Oh dear," said Katarina.

Erik was not taking any chances. He sent eight thousand soldiers after John and Katarina. But John was determined to thwart his half brother. He sailed against those soldiers with only a few hundred men and, amazingly, managed to drive them away. When he saw another ship approaching, he felt sure it came from Poland.

"Your brother has sent us help!" he said to Katarina.

But that ship was also from Sweden and, for reasons known only to himself, John gave up.

"We might as well go see Erik," he said. "Maybe we'll be able to talk some sense into him."

He soon learned that there was little hope of that.

"Since your husband has committed treasonous acts against me, his true king," Erik told Katarina, "your bond of marriage is dissolved. Leave John and you shall go free. Stay with him and you, too, will be a captive."

Katarina looked him right in the eye and held up her wedding ring. On it, in Latin, were engraved the words "Whom God hath joined together."

"I swear before God," said Katarina in a clear, steady voice, "that I will be faithful to John till death us do part."

"Then be a faithful prisoner!" snarled Erik.

For a while, he kept John and Katarina on an island with nothing to protect them from the elements except a simple shelter made from sails. Then he moved them to a shabby apartment in the castle of Gripsholm. Kindly merchants smuggled them money, along with letters from Katarina's sister, Anne, in Poland.

And there Katarina gave birth to her first child, a little girl named Isabella. She bought rags from castle servants so she'd have something to wrap her baby in. Even so, Isabella did not live long. Then Katarina had her second child, a boy called Sigismund. He helped ease the pain caused by the loss of Isabella.

John kept trying to persuade his half brother to give him a proper trial. But Erik would have none of it. Instead, he busied himself thinking up new cruelties with which to torture John. Once he made John ride along a road just outside Stockholm. Gallows lined the road on which hung John's former servants.

Erik had more plans for Katarina, too. It seemed that the tsar of Russia, Ivan the Terrible, wanted to marry her. He would send Erik many fine presents as payment for Katarina. And if Erik refused to give her to him, Russia would attack Sweden.

"Come and get her," said Erik.

To Katarina he said, "Think what great good you will be doing. You will seal the friendship between Sweden and Russia. Eternal glory will be yours. I myself will take you to the border to meet Ivan."

Once again Katarina looked him straight in the eye and said, "No. God help me, no!"

"Perhaps I should just kill John," thought Erik, "and then send Katarina to Ivan. Yes, that might work."

"She is pregnant," John told him. "At least wait until the child is born."

By this time, almost everyone around Erik was horrified, both by what he had done and what he planned to do. People began to protest. That threw Erik into a total rage, and he promptly killed anyone who dared criticize him, including his own son.

Then a man dressed in white appeared before Erik.

"You plan to kill your brother and send his wife to Russia, tyrant," he said. "Well, I say to you that God's anger burns against you. If you do not let your brother and his wife return home, God will take away both your kingdom and your reason. You will wander in the forest as a beast and eat grass as an ox. And you will be damned for all eternity."

With that the man in white disappeared.

"Has anyone entered this room?" Erik asked his attendants.

"Certainly not, Your Majesty," they replied.

"Hmmm," said Erik and immediately sent soldiers to kill John and Sigismund and take Katarina to Russia. They refused.

Then something happened.

"Who is your king?" Erik asked a group of people.

"You, my lord," they replied.

"No, I am not," said Erik. "I am a tyrant." And he took off his clothes and wandered away into the forest. When he was found three days later, he insisted that John become king of Sweden and Finland and Katarina become queen.

"No, no," said John. "Just let us go back to Finland."

But later Erik returned to his evil ways and came up with a plan to murder not only John and Sigismund, but also John's brother Karl and an entire group of nobles. Word of this plan leaked out, and finally even John had had enough. With the help of Karl, he captured Erik and had him thrown into prison. At last his jailer poisoned him with arsenic, and that was the end of Erik.

Meanwhile, John became king of Sweden in 1569 and Katarina became queen. Soon their lives were filled with projects and politics and people. But on an occasional free moment, Katarina must have looked at the words on her wedding ring and smiled. "Whom God hath joined together" no one, not even a mad king, had been able to separate.

*B*oth John and Katarina were well-educated, artistic people, and they brought beauty to Sweden's buildings. Both also wanted to bring Lutheran Sweden back to the Roman Catholic faith. That ensnared them in years of tangles.

"Grief over it all will send me to the grave," said Katarina.

She lived until 1583. Then, after her death, John married a Lutheran woman, and Sweden remained Protestant.

Talk about It

- How do you think the struggles and persecutions Katarina experienced because of being faithful made her feel toward John? Do you think her love grew stronger toward him? Think of marriages today—of people you know and people you know about. How do persecutions, difficulties, and temptations affect the faithfulness of these partners?

- Have each family member vow to do (or not to do) something for the next week that will benefit the whole family. At the end of the week, talk about what it was like to try to keep those vows.

Prayer

Lord, help us to be faithful in large things and in small.
Let us put others before ourselves in all our relationships.
And above all, Lord, keep us faithful to you.
Amen.

The Girl Who Married the Terrible Tsar

ANASTASIA ROMANOV OF RUSSIA
A.D. 1530–1560

 ixteenth-century Russia, known then as Muscovy (MUHSS-kuh-vee), was a land crammed with opposites. Noblemen and merchants decked themselves in velvets and furs and stuffed themselves with rich foods. Peasants, on the other hand, shivered in thin homespun clothing and ate what was left of their crops after they'd surrendered most of them as taxes.

Russian Orthodoxy had long been the state religion, thanks in part to Vladimir, and it had helped introduce advanced ideas from Western civilization. But many primitive and backward customs remained.

Wealthier men and boys could receive an education, but women remained illiterate. Peasants drew their knowledge from their own wits and from ancient superstitions. (Many would go to their grave maintaining that the earth rested on a foundation of seven whales.)

At the age of three, Ivan IV became ruler of this land of contrasts. Others ran the government till he was sixteen, but from then on, Ivan made his own decisions. He decided that he would be known as "tsar," a title similar to "emperor." He decided that execution of his enemies was the best method of controlling them. And he decided to marry Anastasia Romanov. They weren't married long, though, before a terrible disaster occurred.

WHEN ANASTASIA AND IVAN were married in February of 1547, Moscow was a big city with about 200,000 people and more than 40,000 buildings. Unfortunately, most of the buildings were made of wood, and the few streets that weren't mud were paved with logs. On a hill at the center of the city sat the Kremlin, the section where the tsar, his relatives, and a few of the wealthier people lived.

Since she'd come to the tsar's palace, Anastasia had already heard about a couple of fires in the city. With all that wood, primitive cooking methods, and a host of drunks wandering the crooked, narrow streets, the occasional fire seemed almost inevitable. No one knew much about fighting fire either. Mostly people just watched and prayed for help, all the while thinking, "Oh, well, what will be will be."

But no past fire had prepared Anastasia—or the other citizens of Moscow—for the tragedy of June 20, 1547. The flames began, people said, near some wooden churches toward the outer part of the city. Then violent winds seized the flames and hurled them inward, where they gobbled up building after building till they reached the walls of the Kremlin itself. Over the walls they leaped and began licking at the great palaces and cathedrals there.

By this time, of course, Anastasia and Ivan were safely out of the city. Everyone knew that the tsar and tsarina must be rescued at any cost. They retreated, along with others from their court, to a little village in the Sparrow Hills. From there they could look down on Moscow to see what was happening.

To horror-stricken Anastasia it could not have been worse. Wooden buildings simply disappeared. Those few made of stone or brick turned black and crumbled. Mothers screamed for their children, and countless people shoved their way through the streets that led to the Moscow River. If they could jump into the water, they thought, they might be spared. But often their clothes caught fire as they ran, and they never made it to the river.

A messenger brought word that Metropolitan Macarius (mah-KAHR-ee-uss), an important church official and a very old man, had been found praying in the Cathedral of the Assumption inside the Kremlin. His beard was on fire. Other clergy put out the flames and tried to lead him to safety. But he had to climb down a knotted rope, and his tired, old arms weren't equal to it. He fell, lost consciousness, and had to be carried to a monastery nearby.

Trembling, Anastasia stood and prayed for them all.

"Dearest God, help them. Help them, please!" were the only words she could find, but she said them again and again. Anastasia, raised by a widowed mother, had grown up learning to love other people, humble ones as well as great. It was all part of the deep love she felt for Christ. And when other people suffered, she couldn't help but feel their pain, just as her Lord had. But, dear Lord, this was too much—too much pain.

Some instinct for self-preservation took over then, and for a few moments, Anastasia's thoughts drifted away from the ghastly spectacle before her. Instead, she saw the day, not that many months before, when she first came to Moscow. Ivan had announced that he would only marry a Russian girl, and his officials sifted through thousands of prospective brides before finally bringing what they considered the best to the Kremlin. Even then, there were hundreds of young women for Ivan to choose from.

Anastasia would never forget being one of those hundreds, gently herded into a huge house inside the Kremlin walls. There the young women slept twelve to a room while the judging process continued. At times their excitement and nervousness grew to such a pitch that Anastasia wondered if the house might not just explode off its foundations and soar over the walls, never to be seen again. But at times they might also have felt a quiet sort of worry nibbling at them. Ivan was said to be wild and to have a terrible temper. What would life be like married to him?

And all the while, Ivan watched them—when they ate together, when they attended the entertainments put on for them, when they simply sat around talking among themselves. Rumor had it that he even watched them while they slept. He didn't want a wife who snored or tossed and turned and gnashed her teeth.

Eventually Ivan had all but ten of the young women sent away. One night at dinner, he sat beside Anastasia and gave her a ring and a handkerchief embroidered with gold, silver, and pearls.

"He's announcing his decision," thought Anastasia. "He has chosen me!" She turned pink with pleasure.

"I thought I was marrying just because the tsar must have a wife and produce an heir," Ivan told her later. "And then all of a sudden I realized that I loved you! I had never loved anyone before—not like this. I had only hated. But you were so beautiful, so intelligent, so gentle. You *are* all those things. And to me, Anastasia, you will always be my dear little heifer."

Heifer? Anastasia had to smile at that. He would never be smooth, this young tsar of hers. But that didn't matter, because she loved him, too, just as he was. And, oh, how he needed her love! He'd had such a terrible childhood. His father had died when he was three. When he was eight, his mother died, too, probably poisoned by those greedy for power. The nobles responsible for him and his younger brother treated them shabbily, so the little boys were often cold, hungry, and dirty. Once when some people tried to befriend the boys, the power-hungry nobles killed them as the terrified children looked on.

No wonder Ivan had a cruel streak, thought Anastasia. No wonder he thought that killing those who disagreed with him was the best and easiest answer. But never mind. She would make him a home where he knew he was loved no matter what happened in the outside world. She would surround him with her love, her gentleness, and her prayers.

It did not take Anastasia long to realize that the stories of her husband's cruelty were not exaggerated. Sometimes he seemed to turn into a demon who had to hurt and destroy. Anastasia did not want to change the real Ivan—the one who lived deep inside her husband and loved her as she loved him. But she did sometimes wish she could change some of his actions.

As they stood now in the Sparrow Hills looking at the destruction spread out below them, Ivan was raging and reckoning in his mind the monetary value of what he had lost. He felt none of the pain for his people that she felt. Anastasia closed her eyes and returned to her prayers. And to the prayers for the suffering and dying of Moscow, she added prayers for Ivan.

At last the wind died down and so did the fire. There wasn't anything left to burn. But the human misery was far from over. Screams from people buried in the rubble, cries from mourners, and the wails of lost children still filled Moscow's streets the next morning. In all, 1,700 adults had been killed. For some reason, no one counted the children.

Before long, rumors began to spread more quickly than had the flames. People had to blame someone for the tragedy. So they decided that the Glinskys, nobles on Ivan's mother's side of the family, had started the fire. They must be butchered, every one of them. Mayhem overtook the remains of the city. Ivan put down the rebellion of the frenzied people, but it left him shaken.

Then a priest named Sylvester called on Ivan. He said God had sent the fire to punish the tsar for his evil ways. He was very convincing, and Ivan decided at once to become a better person and a better ruler.

First, he took power away from the Glinskys. They were a

troublesome bunch anyway, and his act satisfied the people. Then he set up a council composed of citizens, including Metropolitan Macarius and Sylvester. He gave money to those who had lost everything in the fire and set about having the city rebuilt. It was a good beginning, but deep inside, Ivan sometimes still trembled with fear. During those times, he turned to Anastasia, and she prayed for him and with him.

Finally, Ivan came to a decision. He called representatives from all over Russia to a huge meeting, and there he made a speech. He told the people about his terrible childhood and said it had left him unable to see or hear what his poor subjects needed. But all that had changed. From now on, he and his subjects would live united in Christian love. He would make sure that they all received justice, and he would protect them, too.

The people were thrilled with this magnificent speech. Many even cried. But Anastasia just looked at her husband with glowing eyes. There he stood, the real Ivan, the man she knew he could be. It was a miracle. Her prayers had been answered, and a new and better day was dawning for the Russian people.

*I*van and Anastasia were together for thirteen years. During that time, Anastasia had six children, three of whom died as babies. So many births damaged her health, and she caught a fever the doctors could not cure.

Ironically, as she lay dying, fire again broke out in a part of Moscow near the Kremlin.

After Anastasia's death, Ivan seemed to go mad. His cruelty came rushing back, a thousand times worse than before, and for more than twenty years, Russia suffered unimaginable atrocities. And so, throughout history, this ruler has been known as Ivan the Terrible.

Talk about It

- Talk about Ivan's "terrible-ness." What may have been behind his cruelty? How did Anastasia try to bring out the good side of Ivan? How successful was she? Do you think her methods would work with people today?

- Do you know anyone today who is like Ivan (to a lesser degree, of course)—someone suffering from cruelties experienced during childhood? What could you say or do to help such a person? If you could have talked to Ivan right after Anastasia died, what would you have said to him?

Prayer

Have each family member select some person he or she doesn't particularly like. Then have them pray for that person every night for a month. At the end of the month, talk about this experience. Did you see any difference in the person you were praying for? Did you feel any differently toward that person?

An Old-Fashioned Queen

👑

MARIA THERESA OF AUSTRIA
A.D. 1717–1789

he Hapsburg family had ruled Austria—and much of central Europe—since the thirteenth century. Often, instead of fighting a war for some new territory, they married someone who would bring it to them. Marriage was not nearly as expensive or dangerous as war. But by the time Charles VI became ruler, he found himself with a geographically scattered empire, including what is today Austria, Hungary, a big part of Czechoslovakia, Belgium, Croatia, and bits of Germany, Poland, and Italy.

Charles was not a good ruler. He destroyed the Austrian economy with two senseless wars. Concerned because he had no son, he devised a document stating that his daughter, Maria Theresa, should rule after him and that the Hapsburg lands should continue to belong to the Hapsburgs. Although it was unusual for a woman to inherit her father's throne, Charles got many countries to agree to his document. He hadn't noticed, however, that the breaking of agreements had become quite commonplace in the world around him. And he did absolutely nothing to prepare Maria Theresa for the throne she would someday inherit.

WHEN CHARLES VI DIED, Maria Theresa was twenty-three. She had been married for several years to Francis Stephen, had three little girls, and was pregnant with her fourth child, who would turn out to be a boy.

Although Maria Theresa knew nothing about government, she realized that her father had been a failure. Still, she had loved him dearly and she wept bitterly at his death. In many ways, she felt the same way about her husband, Francis. He had no talent as a military officer and understood government even less than she did. Francis would be of little help to her. But Maria Theresa was always able to love people in spite of their faults.

Now she stood, a lovely young woman with clear blue eyes and hair the color of corn, dressed entirely in mourning. It was her first audience with her government ministers. Although grief still tore at her heart, she had called this audience because she knew she had to. It was her first duty as queen. Behind her was her magnificent throne, but she preferred to stand on the steps that led to it.

"Look at her," whispered one minister to another. "Why, she's only a child."

"Usually a light-hearted little thing, too," replied his companion. "But pale today. Very pale."

Gazing out at them, Maria Theresa thought, "Heavens, how old they all are! Why, some of them were ministers when my *grandfather* ruled! And they look so tired and frightened. I guess that's understandable. I must show them that it truly is a queen who stands before them. Maria Theresa, Queen of Hungary, Queen of Bohemia, Archduchess of Austria, Duchess of Milan, Statthalter of the Netherlands, and all the rest of it."

First, though, she talked about her father and could not keep the tears from her eyes as she did. Then, quite regally, she informed them that they should all retain their appointments for now. Next came a great deal of bowing and hand-kissing, and then it was all over and she could return to her chambers.

"I must think," she told herself as she sank down on a chair and rubbed her aching temples. "God has chosen me for this position, and I must understand my duties as perfectly as I can. My father taught me nothing about the workings of government and statesmanship. In fact, he purposely excluded me from his activities in those areas. To the very end he hoped that somehow, magically, he would have a son. But never mind that. I don't understand finance or war either. But I will! I'll learn about all those things. I have a sacred inheritance now, which I must defend.

"I only wish I had a few—or even *one*—person whose advice I could trust. But I don't, and I might as well face it. The problem isn't that the ministers are old. It's that they never were very good ministers. But I'll bear with them until I find better ones. And above all, I'll do as I have always done—trust in God completely. God has never failed me, and he never will. So I will not go around looking gloomy and tearing out my hair. And," she smiled for the first time since her father had died, "I suspect God doesn't want me to take myself *too* seriously either. After all, he's in charge."

During the first days of her reign, though, it must have seemed that one thundercloud after another rolled down upon her. She had almost no money and no credit. Her army was weak and lacking in morale after her father's poor use of it. Many people were upset and had no trust in her. Some thought Charles Albert of Bavaria would make a much better ruler. Autumn had brought a poor harvest, and the peasants were desperately hungry. Barely had Maria Theresa struggled with one day's problems and fallen into bed when the next day dawned with a whole new batch.

But the greatest blow fell before Maria Theresa had reigned even two months. Frederick II had not sat on the throne of Prussia long, but already he had big plans. People said he was a peaceful man and had strong ties with Austria. They were wrong. Frederick wanted to expand and strengthen Prussia. He wanted to make his own mark on history. In December of 1740, he invaded the Hapsburg land of Silesia.

The battered Austrian army was in no way prepared to defend that country. In April of 1741 they suffered a terrible defeat at a place called Mollwitz. Not one of Austria's allies raised a hand to help. And Maria Theresa felt utterly alone.

"What sort of world is this?" she asked herself. "I believed that allies were loyal to one another. I believed that promises were meant to be kept. I believed in *honor*. Was I wrong about all these things? Am I too old fashioned?"

The fact is that the world was changing. The change had already begun when Charles VI reigned, but Frederick's treacherous act brought it out in the open where everyone could see. From now on, honor would play very little part in the dealings of nations with one another. If they saw something they wanted and were strong enough to take it, they took it. Might now made right.

"No, I wasn't wrong," decided Maria Theresa. "The principles I believe in are right, even if no one else follows them. And I will *not* give up Silesia, at least not all of it. I'll fight as long as I can and then, even if I lose, I know that God will punish my enemies."

Meanwhile, diplomats arrived from Hungary. They invited Maria Theresa to come to Pressburg and be crowned queen.

"Now *that* I will enjoy," she thought. "And heaven knows I could use a little enjoyment about now."

She quickly learned all she could about Hungary and took horseback-riding lessons so she could fulfill her proper part in the ceremony. She had known Count John Palffy, a Hungarian noble, for many years, and he agreed to help her in her dealings with his countrymen.

On the first day, Maria Theresa sailed down the Danube River, escorted by decorated Hungarian barges. Then she was taken to a pavilion set up in a meadow where she changed into a traditional Hungarian costume. After greeting her new subjects, she went by carriage to a palace atop Castle Hill.

The next day, with the help of Palffy and another government official, she managed to have a successful meeting with the Hungarian government. Her Austrian ministers ground their teeth and warned her not to trust those Hungarians. But Maria Theresa knew what she was doing, and the constant carping of officials was beginning to get on her nerves. How sick she was of these self-important men!

In the cathedral she knelt and felt the traditional heavy iron crown of Hungary placed on her head. Then, outside in the cathedral square, she rode a black charger to the top of an artificial mound and pointed her sword north, south, east, and west. That, according to ancient custom, declared her protector of the Hungarian people. The crowds thought she was magnificent.

But soon she had to face the rest of the world again, and it looked stormier than ever. Bavaria, France, and Spain were preparing to attack Austrian land. Frederick had never really stopped. England said it would help, but didn't do much.

"Give in to Frederick," urged the English ministers.

"Do it! Give in," quavered Maria Theresa's own ministers.

"Perhaps you should give in, darling," said her own husband.

Once again Maria Theresa felt utterly alone. Once again she clung to her trust in God. And she had an idea. The people she needed now, the only people who could help her, were the Hungarians. Very well. Why not ask them for their help?

"You wouldn't dare!" gasped her ministers. "Why, to let the Hungarians form an army is simply inviting them to start a revolution against you!"

But Maria Theresa did dare. She traveled to Pressburg again and, with complete honesty, told the Hungarian government what terrible trouble she was in.

"Our safety, and yours, depends on your strength now," she told them.

The Hungarians listened and were impressed. This brave young woman wanted their help. She had come to them in spite of all the mealy-mouthed ministers who tried to stop her. She had shown them respect. They would defend her to the death.

That day Maria Theresa stood a little taller. She had made a big decision, stuck by it, and now knew she was right. She could not count on her allies. Her ministers were totally inept, and most of them despised her. She could never entirely trust her husband either. She could trust only God, and, because of God, she could trust herself. That felt very good.

*E*ventually Maria Theresa found good people to serve as her own ministers and advisors. Though she fought two long wars, she never reclaimed Silesia. But she formed strong bonds with Hungary and Bohemia and made Austria a power to be reckoned with again.

Maria Theresa also improved life for her people. Under her, many more received an education. She changed the tax system to make it more fair. And, when she finally could, she worked for peace.

Maria Theresa died in 1780.

Talk about It

- What did Maria Theresa mean by her decision not to take herself too seriously? Why was she able not to take herself too seriously? How could not taking yourself too seriously make *your* life better?

- Make a list of things that your whole family considers to be important principles. Put a check mark by those that you think most other people believe in, too. Did you include those principles that Maria Theresa lived by?

Prayer

Dear Lord, so many times I worry and fret
and toss and turn. So many times I am tempted
to take myself much too seriously,
forgetting to relax and smile and trust in you.
Teach me to smile and trust.
Remind me that you will always be nearby
to guide and advise and love me,
even when everyone else fails.
Amen.

The Plain Princess

LEOPOLDINA OF BRAZIL
A.D. 1797–1826

*B*razil had supposedly belonged to Portugal since the early sixteenth century, though how such a tiny country could actually own such a huge one was a bit of a mystery. Brazil is the fourth-largest country in the world.

Still, the Portuguese made their presence felt in Brazil. For a while, they tried to make slaves of the Indians, who had lived in Brazil for countless years. When Portuguese priests put an end to that, Africans were brought to serve as slaves instead.

In 1807, Napoleon, ruler of France, invaded Portugal, and the royal family fled for safety to Brazil. They set up court in Rio de Janeiro (ree-oh day zhuh-NAIR-oh) and remained there for fourteen years. During that time, young Prince Dom Pedro (dohm PAY-droh) grew up, and his father decided to find him a wife. Brazil had plenty of wealth in the form of natural resources, mused the king. But it was short on political influence. Now, what country had influence but needed wealth? Austria!

So off went an ambassador to call upon Emperor Francis I and suggest the marriage of Dom Pedro to Francis' daughter, Archduchess Leopoldina (lee-oh-pohl-DEE-nuh). Before long, he was on his way back to Brazil— Leopoldina and several shiploads of European scientists, servants, and other assorted people with him.

"WHAT A STAR-STRUCK LITTLE IDIOT I was back then!" thought Leopoldina as she shoved back her bushy hair with both hands, hoping to feel even the slightest breeze against her skin. "The lovely young princess set sail to join her handsome prince in a fairyland far across the seas. Was it only five years ago? Could I possibly have learned so much in just five years?"

She looked at the portrait of Dom Pedro that the ambassador had given her when he first arrived in Austria. Hanging from a chain of immense Brazilian diamonds, it was framed in diamonds, too, and topped by a crown of still more diamonds.

"Well, he *was* handsome," she thought. "He still is. Handsome and charming and spirited. Perhaps too spirited. . . . No, I won't think about that. The problem is that no lovely young princess came sailing here to join him. Just me. And I've always known that I'm plain and stout. In other words, a dumpling."

Her looks had never bothered Leopoldina before. All her life she had tried to be the sort of person her father wanted her to be, and she had succeeded. Her father adored her.

"My children must rise early and study hard," Emperor Francis had said. And Leopoldina did. She learned to speak English, French, Spanish, Italian, Hungarian, and Czech, as well as German. As she prepared to leave for Brazil, she studied Portuguese, which she correctly concluded was a "difficult language."

Leopoldina also studied history, mathematics, botany, astronomy, Latin, drawing, and music. She especially loved all areas of science, music, and literature.

Francis never let his children forget they were of royal blood. To him, this was no cause for snobbery. Being a ruler meant responsibility, duty, and self-sacrifice. To rule well was more important than to be happy, he taught his children.

Nor did he ignore their religious education. Francis himself was a devout Roman Catholic, and his children followed his lead. When Leopoldina was still in her teens, she joined the Order of the Cross of the Star. This group of laypeople promised to love Jesus Christ, pray, do good deeds, and dress modestly. Leopoldina kept those promises.

So the princess who set sail to join her handsome prince was bright, well-educated, musical, dutiful, and religious. People also described her as kind, with an especially sweet smile. But she was not beautiful.

"Oh, well!" sighed Leopoldina. Then she smiled that sweet smile as her three-year-old daughter, Maria da Gloria, danced into the room. "*You* think your mama is beautiful, don't you *Liebchen*? And I don't think I disappointed the king and queen too terribly."

Once again her mind traveled back to the day of her arrival in Rio de Janeiro. All during her eighty-six-day voyage from Europe, a thread of sadness had woven itself through her excitement.

"I admit that the sacrifice of leaving my family, perhaps forever, is more than painful," she had said, "but God has a particular way of ruling the destinies of us princesses."

As the ships sailed into Rio's beautiful harbor, Leopoldina's excitement overwhelmed her sadness. Cannons were booming and a brass band was playing. There was the king calling out a welcome to her. And there was Dom Pedro, leaping onboard, all decked out in a glittering uniform. Dear God, he was handsome!

Next came the parade when she rode with Dom Pedro in a carriage drawn by eight horses in harnesses of silver and velvet. Bunting and banners lined the road, and the carriage passed through arches made of sweet-smelling flowers. Then came the service in the royal chapel, followed by a huge banquet at the palace. How the crowd cheered her and Dom Pedro as they stood together on the balcony!

But what made Leopoldina feel most welcome was the kindness of her new family. The king put a necklace of four hundred perfect pearls around her neck. The queen slipped diamond and sapphire bracelets on her wrists. The princesses gave her earrings, bangles, a golden pin, and a Spanish comb. Best of all, they soon took her away to their palace in the country.

Rio looked pretty from a distance. But up close it was hot, muggy, and dirty. The stink of the nearby marshes made Leopoldina want to stop breathing, and the sight of the slaves toiling sadly all around made her want to cry.

The country, though, was much better. Here Leopoldina could wander in the forests, collecting rare plants, rocks, and butterflies and watching the birds and monkeys. Before long she started her own small zoo. Brazil would be "a paradise on earth," she decided, if it weren't for "the insufferable heat . . . and the many mosquitoes, which are a veritable torment."

"But I've been fortunate," she thought on that day five years later. "At least I haven't caught any of those terrible diseases that strike down so many foreigners here—yellow fever, malaria, or bubonic plague. Back then I prayed for only one thing to make me completely happy." Again she smiled at her daughter, now playing some game, understood only by herself, on the floor. "And Maria da Gloria was the answer to that prayer. Dom Pedro seems to adore her, too, even if she isn't a boy to inherit the throne."

Sudden tears filled Leopoldina's eyes as they often did these days. She had prayed a long time for a baby boy, and at last a little prince was born. But he didn't live long, and even the birth of another girl couldn't ease Leopoldina's pain.

Meanwhile, Napoleon had been defeated, and the French no longer occupied Portugal. There was no reason the royal family couldn't return. In fact, the Portuguese parliament asked them to—again and again. But the king loved Brazil. He didn't want to go back to all the messy politics he'd find at home.

"You'd better hurry," warned some of the Portuguese politicians. "Otherwise you're going to lose your throne."

So at last the king gritted his teeth and made preparations to return to Portugal. But he would leave Dom Pedro behind to serve as regent in Brazil.

"My father says things are changing here," Dom Pedro told Leopoldina shortly before the king's departure. "He says Brazil is beginning to think of itself as a country in its own right. It won't be satisfied to be governed by Portugal much longer."

Leopoldina nodded. She'd noticed that, too. She was very good at noticing such things, thanks to her father's careful training.

"Parliament wants me to come back to Portugal, too," continued Dom Pedro. "But I don't want to go. Somehow I feel as if I belong here. I feel like a Brazilian."

"You must not go back," said Leopoldina. "Not on my account. Your future is here—and it will be a brilliant one."

Leopoldina firmly pushed all these memories to the back of her mind.

"Now," she thought as she picked up her daughter who had fallen asleep in a heap on the floor, "the day has come. And I'm the one who is going to have to do something about it. God knows I love Dom Pedro, and I try to be a good wife to him. But I have to be honest, too. He is just a bit more interested in having a good time than in being a good ruler. Then there are all the pretty women he can't leave alone. . . . No, I won't think about that. I must save all my wits to persuade him to make his move.

"How ironic, though, that this break with Portugal, which will be such a glorious thing for Brazil, must be such a sad one for me. Because once it has taken place, I can never go home, never see my family again. I will be seen as one of the rebels. Oh, yes, Lord. I understand. It's my duty, one of those sacrifices you expect rulers to make. But it's still very hard."

Trying to look as tall and slim and dignified as she could, she handed Maria da Gloria to a nurse and went to find her husband.

"Darling," she said, "I think it's time."

"Do you?" Dom Pedro looked startled. "I'm not sure if I'm ready yet."

"Of course you're ready," Leopoldina reassured him. "You will make Brazil into a great country. And the people want you to rule them."

"I suppose you're right," said the prince slowly. "Yes, you *are* right! I'll do it. Oh, Leopoldina, you are such a good wife to me."

So Dom Pedro declared that Brazil was now an imperial democracy, and he was Emperor Pedro I. It was all done in a moment. The break with Portugal took place without a drop of blood shed. And in a splendid ceremony on December 1, 1822, Dom Pedro and Leopoldina were crowned emperor and empress of Brazil.

*D*om Pedro became increasingly unfaithful to his wife, a tragedy she dealt with by drawing closer and closer to God. The people knew all she had done for their independence and loved her for it, as well as for her many acts of kindness to the poor. When Leopoldina gave birth to another little prince, their joy was complete.

Leopoldina died after a miscarriage in 1826. She was twenty-nine. Pedro I was as bad a ruler as he was a husband, and after nine years, he was forced to abdicate. Five-year-old Pedro II became emperor and ruled well for many years. One of his acts would have greatly pleased his mother. In 1888, Pedro II abolished slavery in Brazil.

Talk about It

- Leopoldina talked about serving the people she ruled. Why is that a good attitude for any government to have?

- "Duty" is another one of those old-fashioned words. What part do you think the whole idea of duty plays in people's lives today? What part does it play in your life? How do loving God and doing your duty fit together?

Prayer

Dear Lord,
be with all who govern the nations of the world.
Give them the strength and wisdom that they need.
Help them to work for justice, but never forget mercy.
And give them the hearts of servants
who love those they serve.
Amen.

When a *Princess* Said, "*No*"

VICTORIA OF ENGLAND
A.D. 1819–1901

T he threat of insanity hovered over the British monarchy like a great bird of prey. Everyone knew that King George III had been mad for the last ten years of his life. Some said it was the loss of the American colonies that had taken away his reason. After his death, medical investigators suggested that a disease had caused George's problems and he wasn't mad at all.

His son, George IV, was far too fond of food, drink, and fun. By the end of his life, he was so fat he had to be sewn into his clothes each day, and secretly he sometimes wondered if he, too, might be going mad.

William IV was sixty-four when he became king, and he was known as "Silly Billy." He wasn't insane, but he was eccentric. Toward the end of his life, though, William had a goal to which he stuck with all the stubbornness in him. If he lived till his niece Victoria was eighteen, she would rule after him. If he died before then, her mother, the duchess of Kent, would make all decisions for Victoria. William loathed the duchess and determined to live.

Meanwhile, in an apartment in Kensington Palace, young Victoria was growing up in a situation that would have driven many children mad before they came anywhere near the age of eighteen.

FIVE DAYS BEFORE VICTORIA'S eighteenth birthday, the Lord Chamberlain, a high government official, arrived at Kensington Palace. He had, he said, an important message from King William for Princess Victoria.

"Give it to me," said John Conroy, business manager of the Duchess of Kent—Victoria's mother. He reached for the message. "I am used to handling such things."

"Certainly not," said the Lord Chamberlain. "My orders are to give the message to Princess Victoria—no one else."

Once again he tried to hand Victoria the message. This time her mother grabbed at it.

"Madame, *please*," said the Lord Chamberlain, and he firmly placed the message in Victoria's hand.

As Victoria read what the king said, her face remained blank. She was extremely good at showing no expression. She'd had years of practice.

The king, said the letter, wanted to give Victoria three things: an income of 10,000 pounds a year; her own privy purse (a sort of business manager who was answerable only to her); and the right to choose her own ladies-in-waiting.

Without a word, Victoria handed the letter to her mother. It was a marvelous offer, a chance to be free of the duchess and John Conroy forever. But it came five days too soon. Victoria was still under her mother's guardianship. The duchess—with Conroy's help—could do terrible things to make her refuse the offer.

As Conroy and the duchess began raging at William's thoughtlessness and unfairness, Victoria slipped away to her own room.

"Felt very miserable and agitated," she wrote in her journal. "Did not go down to dinner."

The next day Conroy and her mother wrote a reply to the

king's letter, which they told her to sign. It said that she would gratefully accept the 10,000 pounds but felt too young and inexperienced to leave the control of her dear mother.

"I won't sign it," said Victoria. "I want to change it. I want to talk to Lord Melbourne or Mr. Abercromby about it first."

"There is absolutely no need for you to consult anyone else," said Conroy. "We know what is best for you. Sign."

"You know that Sir John is right, Victoria," added her mother. "Sign."

So at last Victoria signed the letter. Then she hurried back to her room and dictated a statement to her beloved governess, Baroness Lehzen. It said that Victoria had not written the reply.

"Only four more days until my birthday," thought Victoria. "Surely I can hold on for four more days. I've held on so long already."

Her thoughts went back to another piece of paper, one that had haunted her the autumn she was sixteen . . .

Her favorite uncle, Leopold, king of Belgium, and his wife Louise, had come for a visit. Victoria so much enjoyed their stay. Uncle Leopold always gave her such good advice. And Queen Louise quickly became like a sister to her. What fun she'd had trying on Louise's fancy Paris gowns!

But too soon it was time for the visitors to leave, and all at once Victoria felt wretched. It was more than exhaustion and sadness that plagued her. Victoria, her doctor announced, had typhoid fever. She could neither eat nor sleep, and high fever cast her into bouts of delirium.

Eventually the plump little princess with long brown ringlets changed into a pitiful little skeleton. Her eyes burned like dark holes in her face, and her hair fell out. More than once her doctor feared she would die. But her faithful governess, Lehzen, remained with her day and night, nursing her and encouraging her.

It was during this, the hardest battle of Victoria's young life, that John Conroy decided to strike. Without an ounce of pity, he marched into her sickroom and ordered her to sign a paper that said he would be her private secretary when she became queen. Victoria refused to sign.

"Leave her alone!" cried Lehzen. "Can't you see how sick she is?"

"Nonsense," replied Conroy. "Victoria, you must sign—and now. It's very important. Someday you will need me, and that must be in writing."

Victoria thrashed her head from side to side and clawed at her covers.

"No," she croaked. No!"

So Conroy went for the duchess.

"Perhaps she will listen to you," he snarled.

"My dear, you must do as Sir John says," murmured Victoria's mother. She didn't even seem to notice how Victoria was suffering. "Sir John knows what is best for you."

The hectoring went on for days as the princess teetered between life and death. Sometimes she felt the cruelty of Conroy's demands and her mother's betrayal pierce through her like swords. Often, though, she simply knew that she must be strong and continue to say no, no matter what they did to her.

After the crisis passed and she began to recover, there was a sadness in Victoria's eyes that did not go away as her hair grew back and she began to put on weight again.

"In my illness I faced the real truth," she told herself now, four days before her eighteenth birthday. "My mother has never loved me. My father died when I was just a baby, and almost at once she fell under Conroy's power. They both knew—long before I did—that someday I would probably be queen; and they wanted to be sure that when that happened, they'd have plenty of money and power. Money and power have been all that mattered to them.

"I wonder if anyone has ever loved me. Lehzen, perhaps, and dear old Baroness Spath, whom Conroy sent away. Dear God, Conroy has controlled my whole life. He even saw to it that his children were the only friends I was allowed—and nasty little beasts they were, too. Anything I said, any expression on my face was reported to him and my mother. And when I was old enough to keep a journal, my mother openly read that—and probably discussed it with Conroy. No wonder I've felt so crushed and kept under. No wonder I have learned to keep my face a blank."

But in spite of the dark cloud that had covered most of her childhood, Victoria couldn't help but remember some bright spots, too. The fun of doing arithmetic. Her music and dancing lessons. Drawing—at which she was rather talented. And her dolls.

Victoria and Lehzen had wonderful times together dressing little ceramic dolls in scraps of finery. Then Victoria would dream up names and personalities for them. Mothers, fathers, and children; ballet dancers, actors, and opera singers. The adventures she invented for her dolls brought color to little Victoria's drab days.

Then there were the animals: first her pony, Rosa, and her dog, Fanny; later the parakeet, the canary, and the black spaniel, Dash, who had been given to her mother but who quickly became Victoria's dog and dearest friend.

"Dogs love you no matter what happens," she thought. "I shall always have a dog."

"And God," she thought. "Where would I be if I couldn't rely on God's love? For most people, going to church seems just to be a duty. But I honestly like it. And I like sermons, especially the cheerful ones. They give me strength to face the week ahead. I guess my favorite text is 'Behold, now is the day of salvation.' Maybe it reminds me that my eighteenth birthday is coming. Oh dear! Is that a blasphemous way to think?"

At last the day came. May 24 and Victoria was officially

eighteen years old. Congratulations and best wishes showered on her from all around. The king held a ball for her and gave her a grand piano. Victoria herself was filled with resolution.

"I shall from this day… strive to become every day less trifling and more fit for what, if Heaven wills it, I'm someday going to be," she wrote in her journal.

But for a while it seemed to Victoria that not much had changed. She still lived with her mother, and Conroy still pressured her to sign that paper making him her private secretary. When she continued to refuse, Conroy began telling people that she was mentally unstable. Insanity again? Could it be?

Then, very early on the morning of June 20, the Lord Chamberlain and the Archbishop of Canterbury, head of the Church of England, came to Kensington Palace with news for her. King William was dead. She was now Queen Victoria.

She received the news quietly and quietly went about the business of the next few days. Many people were astonished at the dignity of this eighteen-year-old girl and how smoothly she took on her duties as monarch of one of the world's most powerful nations.

Of course those duties so occupied her time that she couldn't see her mother very often. And the quiet, dignified young queen must have shouted a few alleluias deep in her soul when she issued the decree that all Conroys were to be kept away from the palace. A day of salvation indeed!

*V*ictoria ruled England for sixty-three years during a period when the British Empire included about twenty-five percent of the land and people in the world. Although vast changes swept society during her reign (and not always for the better) and wars plagued her empire, Victoria found a place in the hearts of her people. She also found the love denied her in childhood in the person of Albert, a German prince, her husband and best friend.

Talk about It

- Unfortunately too many children today don't know what it is like to be loved by a parent either. Do you know any such children? How might your family befriend them?

- Think of an older person in your extended family or neighborhood that might not experience as much love as he or she could use—perhaps a widowed aunt or grandmother. Talk about ways you could show that person more love on a regular basis. Then ask God to help you do it—from now on.

Prayer

Dear Lord,
be with all those people who especially need love—
the old people, the lonely people, and the little children.
Fill them with your love so they never feel entirely alone.
And help us to show them your love and ours
through our words and actions.
Amen.

The Disobedient Chief

KHAMA OF BECHUANALAND
A.D. 1828–1923

*P*icture a map of Africa. Go up a little bit from the bottom (that's South Africa) and make a dot. Then draw a small circle around the dot, leaving plenty of room on both sides. That, very roughly, is today's Republic of Botswana.

Cattleherders from the Tswana (suh-WAH-nuh) tribes moved down from the north and into this territory almost a thousand years ago. There they fought the Nguni (uhn-GOO-nee) tribes and the Bushmen who already lived there. They won. Today people from the Tswana tribes form about ninety-five percent of Botswana's population.

Some of their tribes were known as the Bechuana (bet-choo-WAH-nuh), and most powerful of the Bechuana was the Bamangwato (bah-mang-WAH-toh) tribe. In the early nineteenth century, it was ruled by Chief Sekhome (seck-HOH-mee), a cruel man who kept his people firmly under his thumb. Not only was Sekhome their warrior-chief, he was also a witch doctor whom they believed could control their very spirits.

But in 1828, something softened in Chief Sekhome for just a moment. His first son was born. And as he looked at the wailing infant, Sekhome smiled. "He will rule after me," he said to himself. "Khama (KAH-muh)— my Khama."

KHAMA WAS NOT AFRAID of his father the way everyone else was. Even as a tiny child, he knew that Sekhome loved him and was proud of him. He'd do anything to keep him safe. And, growing up in the royal village, or *kraal* (KRAHL), Khama did feel safe. The huts of the kraal had been built in a large circle, all facing toward the big open space in the middle, as was the custom. Behind them rose a high fence. On the other side of that fence, Khama knew, roamed dangerous wild animals and sometimes warriors from enemy tribes. The fence protected them—and Khama.

So did his father's soldiers and witch doctors. The soldiers were fine, strong warriors and the witch doctors claimed to know a great deal about how to control evil spirits. So Khama didn't really have to be afraid of anything. He could just concentrate on growing up to be a mighty chief like his father.

But then one day when Khama was about fourteen, Sekhome sent for him.

"I have heard strange rumors, my son," he said; and if Khama hadn't known better, he would have thought he saw something like fear in his father's eyes.

"There is a man coming toward us through the forests," continued Sekhome, "a white man. And they say that nothing—no animal, no disease, no person—frightens him."

"What are you going to do, Father?" asked Khama.

"It is better to face the unknown than to fret about it," replied Sekhome. "So I am taking my warriors and going out to meet this man. I want you to come with me."

Khama's chest swelled out till he thought it might pop. So! Now his father felt he was old enough to confront the enemy instead of hiding in safety like a child. Well, he would show Sekhome that he was right.

But when they came upon the white man, Khama realized immediately that he was no enemy. A big smile covered his face and his eyes glowed with kindness and compassion.

"My name is David Livingstone," he said, "and I have come to bring you good news."

"What good news can this white man have for us?" thought Khama. He didn't have long to wonder. Soon Livingstone was telling them stories about someone called Jesus, someone who was the Son of the one true God. This Jesus, said Livingstone, had come to earth many years ago. Here he lived and taught and healed. Then he had let his enemies kill him, but his Father had raised him from the dead again—and all so that people could become children of the one true God forever.

"The one true God?" asked Khama. "Aren't there many gods? Our witch doctors say so. Was this Jesus a witch doctor too?"

"No, no, no," replied Livingstone, and he went on to tell more about Jesus and the Father in heaven who had sent him. As Livingstone talked, Khama felt himself liking him more and more. And he felt strangely drawn toward the one called Son of God.

Sekhome, meanwhile, paid little attention to what Livingstone said. But he was very impressed by the fact that he couldn't frighten the white man. There weren't many people Sekhome couldn't frighten, so from then on he treated Livingstone with respect and allowed him to travel unhindered through the Bechuanas' land.

Years passed and Khama continued to grow. After a while, his fellow tribesmen began calling him "Khama the Antelope" because he was so tall and strong and ran so swiftly. Khama was brave, too. Once he killed a lion; and he fought as fiercely as anyone against enemy warriors.

"You're just like me," his father told him. "And someday you also will be a great chief."

But Khama wasn't just like his father. The stories David

Livingstone had told him about Jesus remained in a special place in his heart. And he longed to learn more about God's Son.

His chance came when another chief invited the young man to come and stay with him for a while. This chief had also met David Livingstone and, through him, had become a Christian.

"I have so many questions!" Khama told him.

"I know," said the chief. "And I will answer as many as I can. But I will also teach you how to read and write. Those skills will help you find your own answers."

When Khama returned to his father's village, he was a different young man. He was still as swift and strong and brave as ever. But he had given his heart to Jesus and somehow, he knew, that would change his whole life.

"Father, I would like you to let a white missionary come to our people," he said.

"You mean that Livingstone fellow?" asked Sekhome.

"Not him, but someone like him," said Khama. "It would do our people so much good, Father. I promise you that."

"Well . . . all right," said Sekhome. "I'd like to know a little more about this magic whatever-it-is myself."

So the missionary came, and many of the Bamangwato people listened and learned from him. In 1860, at the age of thirty-two, Khama became a baptized Christian. So did his younger brother.

By then Sekhome was growing old. However his cruelty still burned strong in him. He had not taken to the missionary and his teachings at all.

Furthermore, this new religion had taught Khama disobedience. When Sekhome wanted him to marry many wives—as any powerful chief should—Khama said no. He had married his one wife, his beloved Ma-Bessie, and she was all he wanted.

"And if that isn't bad enough," raged Sekhome, "now he refuses to join in the witch doctors' dances and feasts. He says they're savage and evil and that he believes only in the one true God. Well, he's no longer a son of mine. I hate him!"

So Sekhome sent for his most clever and powerful witch doctors and ordered them to put a spell on Khama.

"Make it a strong spell," he said, his voice cold with fury, "the strongest you have. I want Khama to die."

Night came and Khama lay in his hut, asleep with Ma-Bessie. All at once he woke up. What was that noise? Voices muttered just outside the hut and—yes—he heard flames crackling.

Silent as an antelope, Khama slipped outside. There they hunkered, the head witch doctors, swaying back and forth around the fire and mumbling hideous spells—against him!

"We'll see how powerful their pitiful little spells are against a child of the one true God," thought Khama. He leaped from the shadows right at the witch doctors.

"Aieeeeee!"

In an instant the witch doctors were gone, running as fast as their shaking legs would carry them. Khama just smiled as he stamped out their fire.

He knew, though, that neither he nor his brother would be safe as long as Sekhome was alive. The old man would not give up so easily. Somehow, by trickery if not by outright confrontation, he'd find a way to kill his despised Christian sons.

"We must hide in the hills," Khama told his brother, "until our father dies. But it will not be so bad. We will have each other. And God will watch over us."

When at last, in 1872, Sekhome died, the Bamangwato people did not hesitate. They did not always understand Khama and his strange Christian ways, but they knew that they wanted him to be their next chief. So they gave him the royal leopard skin to wear and looked to him to lead them.

And that is exactly what Khama did. He didn't force the people to give up witchcraft and the cruel customs that went with it. Instead, he showed them by his own behavior how much better life could be without these things.

Another evil that constantly tempted the Bamangwato was the crude liquor sold to them by white traders.

"I won't have you selling my people that poison anymore," Khama told the traders.

But the traders ignored him, and the drunkenness continued. So Khama sent for the traders and told them in no uncertain terms that they must leave his country—period. They left.

The people mumbled and grumbled for a while. But once again they eventually understood that Khama was right.

The next evil came from the south—white men looking for gold and diamonds. They offered the Bamangwato fat bribes, and Khama feared that his people would sell away all their land. Greed was a powerful enemy—much worse than witch doctors— and Khama did not think he could fight it, or the evil gold and diamond merchants alone. So in 1885, he wrote to Queen Victoria in England, asking her to join him in protecting his people.

The queen agreed and, at the request and consent of Khama, Bechuanaland became a British protectorate, a state under Britain's power and authority.

Khama died in 1923, and his people mourned him deeply. Bechuanaland remained a British protectorate until 1966 when it became the republic of Botswana, a multi-party democratic state. Although Botswana is still a poor country with cattle its chief economic asset, its rich deposits of diamonds and other minerals promise the country a much brighter future. Khama would have liked that.

Talk about It

• Why do you suppose Sekhome had so much trouble accepting things the missionaries taught? What were some things that might have kept Khama from continuing to believe David Livingstone's message of good news? What things might keep people you know from accepting the Christian faith?

• Many people know almost nothing about the country of Botswana. What are some of the most important things you would tell them about the country? Choose several up-to-date resources from your neighborhood or school library to learn more about the country today. How have things changed since the days of Khama? What part do Christians play in the life of the country?

Prayer

Dear Lord,
we are all so different, yet all so much the same—
all children of the one true God. Help us to feel the bond
of your love uniting us all around the world.
Let us never forget that you made us all, redeemed us all,
and sustain us all with your Spirit. We pray in Jesus' name.
Amen.